REFRESHING AND DELICIOUS
PUNCH RECIPES

TERRY TAILOR

CONTENTS

➤JUNE BUG PUNCH

Yield 1 Servings

- ❖ 2 pk kool-aid,lime or any red-flavor
- ❖ 2 c sugar
- ❖ 46 oz can pineapple-grapefruit-juice
- ❖ 1 water
- ❖ 1 juice of 1 lemon,optional
- ❖ 1 mint leaves,optional

In a gallon container, add Kool-Aid, sugar and juice. Fill up the rest of the container with water; add lemon juice. Refrigerate or serve over ice.

Punch may be frozen in ice trays for flavored ice cubes. Garnish with mint leaves in each glass for extra flair.

➤JUNGLE JUICE PUNCH

Yield 0 Servings

- ❖ 1 1/2 qt water

- ❖ 4 c sugar

- ❖ 1   46-ounce can pineapple juice

- ❖ 1   46-ounce can orange juice

- ❖ 1/4 c lemon juice

- ❖ 6 ripe bananas,mashed

- ❖ 2   32-ounce bottles ginger ale,chilled

Combine water and sugar in a large Dutch oven. Bring to a boil; cook 5 minutes or until sugar dissolves, stirring frequently. Let mixture cool slightly. Add juices and mashed banana, stirring well. Transfer juice mixture to a freezer container; cover and freeze at least 8 hours.

To serve, let stand at room temperature 4 to 5 hours or until slushy. Gently stir in ginger ale just before serving.

➤JUNIPER'S GIN PUNCH

Yield 18 Servings

- ❖ 1 stephen ceideburg
- ❖ 1 orange
- ❖ 2 limes
- ❖ 1 water
- ❖ 3 c gin, chilled
- ❖ 2 c apricot brandy, chilled
- ❖ 2 l club soda, chilled
- ❖ 12 oz orange juice, Frozen-concentrate

Slice the orange and limes into thin round slices and line a 4 cup round mold with the slices. Carefully fill the mold with cold water and place in the freezer. Freeze until solid.

Combine gin, brandy, club soda, orange juice concentrate and stir to blend in a punch bowl. Unmold the ice ring and carefully float it in the punch bowl, fruited side up.

➤KAHLUA PARTY PUNCH

Yield 1 Servings

- ❖ 2 c kahlua

- ❖ 12 oz apple juice concentrate

- ❖ 1/2 c lemon juice

- ❖ 25 oz apple juice

- ❖ 1 5th dry champagne

- ❖ 1 qt lemon lime soda (or club)soda

- ❖ 1 ice

- ❖ 1 lemon,Slices

- ❖ 1 orange,Slices

Chill all ingredients well. Combine kahlua with undiluted apple juice concentrate and lemon juice. Pour over a small chunk of ice in punch bowl. Add sparkling apple juice, soda and champagne; stir gently. Garnish with thin lemon and orange slices. Makes 30, 1/2 cup servings.

➤LIME LEMON PUNCH

Yield 100 Servings

- ❖ 1 1/2 ga water, cold

- ❖ 1 1/2 ga water, hot

- ❖ 3 ga ice

- ❖ 12 lb. lemon fresh

- ❖ 7 lb. sugar, granulated

- ❖ 10 lb 1 t imitation lemon flavor

1. USE GRANULATED SUGAR.

2. USE CANNED FROZEN, SINGLE STRENGTH LIME JUICE AND WATER. ADD GREEN FOOD COLORING.

3. ADD ICE JUST BEFORE SERVING.

➤LIME PARTY PUNCH

Yield 16 Servings

- ❖ 1 pk (4-serving size) Jell-O-brand gelatin, lime flavor 1 pk (4-serving size) Jell-O-brand gelatin, lemon flav 2 c water, Boiling

- ❖ 1bottle (1 liter) club soda-lemon soda (or lemon-lime) 1 c white wine (optional)

- ❖ 1orange, lemon or lime-thinly sli

- ❖ 1 ice cubes (optional)

DISSOLVE gelatins in boiling water; cool. (Keep at room temperature until ready to serve.) Stir in club soda, wine and orange slices just before serving. Serve over ice, if desired.

MAKES 8 cups or 16 servings

➤LIME PUNCH

Yield 1 Servings

- ❖ 1 2 liter bott sprite
- ❖ 1/2 ga lime Sherbet

Pour in punch bowl that has been chilled. Garnish with lemon and lime slices and cherries if desire color.

➤LIZA'S LEMONADE PUNCH

Yield 1 Servings

- ❖ 1   12 oz can white grape juice, Frozen

- ❖ 1   12 oz can lemonade, frozen

- ❖ 1 l club soda

Unthaw and blend juices in punch bowl. Add club soda just before serving. Make ice cubes (or use a ring mold) out of reconstituted lemonade or orange juice and place in punch at serving time. This keeps the punch cool without diluting it. Slice oranges, lemons or limes and place those in the ring mold for decoration too.

➤LONDON TOWN GRATITUDE PUNCH

Yield 1 Servings

- ❖ 1 c tang

- ❖ 1/2 c sugar

- ❖ 2/3 c tea powder, Instant

- ❖ 3 oz pkg wyler lemonade mix

- ❖ 1/2 t cinnamon, Ground

- ❖ 1/4 t cloves, Ground

Combine all ingredients. Use two tablespoons per cup of boiling water. 2 oz rum may optionally be added per cup.

➤MAGICAL PARTY PUNCH

Yield 1 Servings

- ❖ 1 assorted colors liquid food-colorin,
- ❖ 1 pineapple juice
- ❖ 1 orange juice
- ❖ 1 red fruit punch
- ❖ 1 lemon-lime soft drink-chilled

Stir desired amount of food coloring into separate juices. Pour juices and fruit punch into separate ice trays. Freeze. To serve, pour chilled soft drink over 3 to 4 assorted cubes.

➤MALIHINI PUNCH

Yield 8 Servings

- ❖ 1 qt orange juice

- ❖ 1/2 c lilikoi syrup

- ❖ 1/2 c guava syrup

- ❖ 1 ice cubes

Combine orange juice, lilikoi syrup and guava syrup; blend well. Chill. Serve over ice cubes.

➤MANGO PUNCH

Yield 1 Servings

- ❖ 1 c sugar

- ❖ 1/4 c white rum

- ❖ 1 doz ripe mangos

- ❖ 3 qt water

Wash mangos and peel them, rub through sieve. Add water and bring to quick boil. Simmer for about 1/2 hour. Allow to cool, then add rum and sweeten. Serve chilled.

➤MARCELLES MILK PUNCH

Yield 1 Servings

- ❖ 1 c sugar
- ❖ 1 c water
- ❖ 2 c bourbon
- ❖ 2 c brandy
- ❖ 3 qt half and half
- ❖ 4 T vanilla extract
- ❖ 1 simple syrup
- ❖ 1 nutmeg, Grated

For the simple syrup in a small sauce pan, combine the sugar and water. Stir and boil until the sugar dissolves and the liquid becomes a slight syrup. Cool the syrup before using. Makes 1 cup. Set the syrup aside.

In a glass container, combine the bourbon, brandy, half and half, and vanilla, together. Stir the liquid until incorporated. Stir in the syrup to your own desired sweetness. Chill the punch well. Serve the punch in chilled glasses and garnish with nutmeg.

➤MARTHA HYER'S COFFEE PUNCH

Yield 15 Servings

- ❖ 1 qt strong coffee
- ❖ 2 c milk, cold
- ❖ 2/3 T vanilla
- ❖ 1/2 c sugar
- ❖ 1 qt vanilla ice cream
- ❖ 1 c stiffly whipped cream
- ❖ 1 nutmeg

Combine coffee, milk, vanilla, and sugar. Stir until sugar is dissolved. Chill until serving time. Place ice cream in a punch bowl. Pour coffee over ice cream. Pour whipped cream on top of mixture. Dust lightly with nutmeg as each cup is served.

15

➤MARTY'S YELLOW PUNCH

Yield 1 Servings

- ❖ 1 lg packag lemon jello

- ❖ 1 cn frozen orange juice,(12-oz.)

- ❖ 1 cn frozen pink lemonade, (12-oz.)

- ❖ 1 cn pineapple juice, (46 oz.)

Mix Jell-O according to directions on package. In a large container, mix Jell-O and fruit juices. Add amount of water on each can. You can use any flavor Jell-O for color. Makes approximately 5 quarts. Can also be frozen for a slush.

➤MELE KALIKIMAKA PUNCH

Yield 1 Servings

- ❖ 1 can cranberry juice, Frozen
- ❖ 1 concentrate
- ❖ 1 cn lemonade concentrate,Frozen
- ❖ 2 l lemon-lime soda
- ❖ 1 bottle sparkling mineral
- ❖ 1 water
- ❖ 1 pk raspberries, Frozen

You know how to mix.

➤MERRY MARY PUNCH

Yield 24 Servings

- ❖ 1 bottle Tabasco brand -Extra-Spicy Bloody Ma

- ❖ 1 1/2 qt orange juice

- ❖ 1 c Lemon juice (juice of 6-lemons)

- ❖ 2 T Sugar

- ❖ 2 c Gin, vodka (or rum),or to-taste

In a large bowl, mix all ingredients well. Refrigerate until ready to serve. Pour into punch bowl with large block of ice or decorative ice float. This recipe yields 24 servings.

➤MEXICAN SUNRISE PUNCH

Yield 6 Servings

- ❖ 1 cn orange juice concentrate
- ❖ 1 cn lemonade concentrate
- ❖ 1 cn limeade concentrate
- ❖ 9 c water
- ❖ 2/3 c tequila
- ❖ 1 cn ginger ale (12 oz.)
- ❖ 1 grenadine syrup (optional)
- ❖ 1 lime slices, for garnish
- ❖ 1 ice cubes

Put frozen juices in a medium-size punch bowl or large pitcher. Stir in water. Add tequila, ginger ale, and if desired, about 1/4 cup grenadine. Add ice; stir again. Garnish with lime slices. Makes 12 cups.

➤MEXICAN TEA PUNCH

Yield 8 Servings

- ❖ 1 c tequila
- ❖ 2 c tea, strong, cold
- ❖ 1 c pineapple juice
- ❖ 1/4 c honey
- ❖ 1/4 c water
- ❖ 1/4 c lime juice
- ❖ 1/4 c lemon juice
- ❖ 1 1/2 t cinnamon, ground
- ❖ 1 1/2 t aromatic bitters

Mix all ingredients; refrigerate until chilled. Stir before serving. Serve over ice.

➤MIMI'S PUNCH

Yield 8 Servings

- ❖ 1 pk raspberry kool-aid
- ❖ 1 c sugar
- ❖ 1 cn minute maid lemonade,Frozen-concentrate
- ❖ 1 cn pineapple juice,unsweetened
- ❖ 1 (64 oz.)
- ❖ 2 qt ginger ale,canada dry
- ❖ 2 qt cold water

Mix Kool-Aid and sugar together with 1-3/4 quarts of water. Add lemonade concentrate and remaining water. Mix thoroughly and freeze until hard. Remove from freezer, chip and store. When ready to serve, combine chipped ice with chilled ginger ale and pineapple juice.

➤MINT PUNCH

Yield 1 Servings

- ❖ 1 c water
- ❖ 1 c granulated sugar
- ❖ 1 c fresh mint leaves,or you can substitute
- ❖ 6 bigelow mint medley tea bags
- ❖ 1 c orange juice
- ❖ 1 c lemon juice
- ❖ 2 ga slice (or 7-up)

Bring water and sugar to a boil, boil for 5 minutes.

Place mint in a cheesecloth and pir above mixture over mint, or use the tea bags

Add orange juice and lemon juice, and place in a cooler for at least 4 hours.

Add soda just before serving. Serve over crushed ice.

➤MINT RASPBERRY PUNCH

Yield 1 Servings

- ❖ 1/4 c orange juice
- ❖ 1/2 c lemon juice
- ❖ 1/2 c sugar
- ❖ 1 T raspberry flavoring
- ❖ ½ dozen sprigs fresh mint
- ❖ 1 pt cold water

Mix fruit juices, sugar and raspberry powder or flavor. Stir well and add water. Pour over large pieces of ice. Serve with a sprig of mint in each glass.

➤MINT-FALVORED PUNCH

Yield 1 Servings

- ❖ 2/3 c sugar
- ❖ 1/2 c fresh mint,Lightly Packed
- ❖ 1 leaves,snipped
- ❖ 2 c red grape juice,chilled
- ❖ 2 c orange juice,chilled
- ❖ 3/4 c lime juice,chilled
- ❖ 1 ice,Crushed
- ❖ 1 fresh mint leaves

Combine sugar, mint, & 2 c. boiling water; stir till sugar dissolves.

Chill. Strain, reserving liquid; discard leaves. Stir together reserved liquid, grape juice, orange juice & lime juice. Serve over crushed ice. Garnish with fresh mint leaves.

➤MINTED PUNCH

Yield 8 Servings

- ❖ 5 c water

- ❖ 6 whole cloves

- ❖ cinnamon stick - (3" to 4")

- ❖ 1 T ginger root,Minced

- ❖ 1/2 c fresh mint leaves,Chopped

- ❖ 1 whole mint leaves,for garnish

- ❖ 2 1/2 c sugar

- ❖ 1 lemon,cut in half

In large saucepan over medium heat, stir together water, cloves, cinnamon stick, ginger and mint. Bring mixture to boil, reduce heat to medium and simmer, uncovered, until liquid is reduced to 4 cups, about 15 minutes. Add sugar and stir until dissolved.

Remove from heat. Squeeze juice from half of lemon into punch and mix well. Strain punch into pitcher or punch bowl; discard solids. Thinly slice other lemon half and add to punch. Serve punch warm or cold; to serve cold, cover tightly and chill 2 hours to overnight.

➤MISSISSIPPI WEDDING PUNCH

Yield 50 Servings

- ❖ 1 cn (46-oz) pineapple juice

- ❖ 2 cn (6-oz) orange juice,Frozen

- ❖ 2 cn (6-oz) lemon juice,Frozen

- ❖ 1 c sugar,very scant

- ❖ 1 fifth champagne (up to)

- ❖ 4 qt ginger ale

Mix juices and sugar and add enough water to make 1 gallon. Just before serving, stir in champagne and ginger ale. (If frozen lemon juice cannot be obtained, use frozen lemonade and omit sugar).

➤MOCHA PUNCH

Yield 20- Servings

- ❖ 1 1/2 qt water

- ❖ 1/2 c chocolate drink mix,Instant

- ❖ 1/2 c sugar

- ❖ 1/4 c coffee granules,Instant

- ❖ 1/2 ga vanilla ice cream

- ❖ 1/2 ga chocolate ice cream

- ❖ 1 c whipped cream,whipped

- ❖ 1 c chocolate curls,optional

In a large saucepan, bring water to a boil. Remove from the heat. Add drink mix, sugar and coffee; stir until dissolved. Cover and refrigerate for 4 hours or overnight. About 30 minutes before serving, pour into a punch bowl. Add ice cream by scoopfuls; stir until partially melted. Garnish with servings (about 5 quarts).

➤MOCK CHAMPAGNE PUNCH

Yield 12 Servings

- ❖ 10 oz strawberries in syrup sliced and Thawed

- ❖ 2 cn peach nectar (or apricot) -5.5 - oz. each

- ❖ 1/4 c lemon juice

- ❖ 2 T honey

- ❖ 2 bottles white wine

- ❖ -sparkling (or white grape)

- ❖ 1 pt strawberry (or raspberry) -sorbet

- ❖ 1 fresh strawberries,sliced

- ❖ 1 fresh mint sprigs,optional

Place strawberries with syrup in blender container or food processor; blend until smooth. Pour mixture into large picture. Stir in peach or apricot nectar, lemon juice and honey; blend well. Refrigerate until serving time. To serve, pour mixture into large punch bowl. Stir in sparking wine or white grape juice. Drop small scoops of sorbet into punch. If desired, garnish with sliced strawberries and mint.

➤MOCK MARGARITA PUNCH

Yield 24 Servings

- ❖ 1 (12-oz) can lemonade,Frozen
- ❖ Concentrate,thawed
- ❖ 1 (12-oz) can limeade,Frozen
- ❖ 2 Concentrate,thawed
- ❖ 1 c Powdered sugar
- ❖ 4 Whole smilin' egg whites
- ❖ 6 c ice,Crushed
- ❖ 1 Quart (4-cups) club soda
- ❖ Chilled
- ❖ Lime,Slices
- ❖ Coarse salt

In 4-quart not-metal container, combine lemonade and limeade concentrates, powdered sugar, egg whites and crushed ice; mix well. Cover; freeze, stirrinc occasionally. Remove container from freezer 30 minutes before serving. Spoon 2 cups slush mixture into blender;

add 1 cup club soda.

Cover; blend until frothy. to serve, rub rim of glass with lime slice and dip in coarse salt; fill glass. Garnish with lime slices.

YIELD 24 (1/2-cup) servings

➤MOM'S PUNCH

Yield 3 Servings

- ❖ 1 1/2 qt cans of cranberry juice
- ❖ 4 6 oz. cans lemonade,Frozen
- ❖ 1 mold with any fruit juice
- ❖ 2 qt ginger ale
- ❖ 1 qt sherbet (any flavor)

Mix cranberry juice and lemonade in punch bowl, place frozen mold in center and add 1 bottle of ginger ale, then add sherbet. Add the rest of ginger ale. Lemon or lime sherbet makes a tart punch.

➤MONARCHY LUAU PUNCH

Yield 30 Servings

- ❖ 1 fresh pineapple
- ❖ 1/2 c brandy
- ❖ 2 T sugar
- ❖ 3 c pineapple juice
- ❖ 1/2 ga white wine
- ❖ 1 qt champagne

Remove rind and core form pineapple; coarsely chop fruit. Combine pineapple, brandy and sugar; marinate 6 hours or overnight. Pour pineapple juice into a ring mold and freeze. Add wine to pineapple-brandy mixture; refrigerate 30 minutes. Add pineapple juice ring and champagne just before serving.

➤MOOSEMILK PUNCH

Yield 20 Servings

- ❖ 6 eggs
- ❖ 113 g caster sugar
- ❖ 2 l milk
- ❖ 1 l vanilla ice cream,partially ,Melted
- ❖ 600 ml dark rum
- ❖ 400 ml brandy
- ❖ 400 ml tia maria
- ❖ 1 freshly-grated nutmeg

Separate the egg yolks and whites into separate bowls. Add the sugar to the yolks and beat until frothy. Beat the whites until they form peaks. Combine the yolk and white mixtures and add with the milk to the ice cream. Add the rum, brandy and Tia Maria last. Serve sprinkled with nutmeg.

➤MULLED CINNAMON BASIL PUNCH

Yield 4 Servings

- ❖ 4 c apple juice
- ❖ 1/4 c sugar
- ❖ 1/3 c cinnamon basil leaves (or -to) taste
- ❖ 1/2 t whole cloves
- ❖ 2 limes,thinly sliced

Heat applejuice, sugar, cinnamon basil, cinnamon stick and cloves, stirring until mixture comes to a boil. Reduce heat, stir in limes and simmer 5 minutes. Strain into mugs and serve hot, or cool and serve over ice for a cold drink.

➤MYSTERY PUNCH

Yield 1 Servings

- ❖ 1/4 c lemon juice

- ❖ 1 t ginger,Ground

- ❖ 2 qt cider (or apple juice)

- ❖ 3 c water

- ❖ 1 cn (12 ounces) orange,Frozen
  -juice concentrate

- ❖ 1 hand (see below),Frozen

- ❖ FROZEN HAND

- ❖ 1 ed,blue or green food
  -coloring

- ❖ 1 water

- ❖ 1new disposable plastic or rubber glove

DIRECTIONS In a large pitcher or glass gallon jar; stir lemon juice and ginger until blended. Add cider, water and orange juice concentrate and stir until blended. Cover and chill at least 1 hour.

To serve, place punch in a large, chilled punch bowl. Add frozen hand or ice ring. Ladle into punch cups.

FROZEN HAND Add food coloring to water until you reach desired color.

Fill glove with colored water, fastening end with a twist tie or rubber band. Hang glove from a shelf in the freezer and freeze overnight. When frozen, remove glove from ice and place "hand" in the punch.

➤MYSTIC PUNCH

Yield 1 Servings

- ❖ 1ice cubes with raisins frozen in them

- ❖ 4 bottles (1-pint) cranberry juice

- ❖ 2 1/2 c juice from 2 (1-pound -14-ounce) cans of spiced

- ❖ 1 c fresh lime juice (about 8 limes)

- ❖ 2 c orange juice

- ❖ 1sugar,To Taste

Keep the juices refrigerated until you are ready to use them. In a punch bowl, combine all the juices. Add the ice cubes and serve.

MAKES 20 CUPS

➤NANCY'S PARTY PUNCH

Yield 1 Servings

- ❖ 1 qt Ginger Ale
- ❖ 12-Oz Can Lamonade,Frozen
  -Concentrate,thawed
- ❖ 2 c Water
- ❖ 2 c Cranberry Juice.
- ❖ Ice Cubes

Well before serving time, freeze water in a large Cool Whip or Similar container to make a large ice cube. (I sometimes use a pretty-shaped mold.)

Just before serving, mix together ginger ale, lemonade, 2 cups water, and cranberry juice in a large punch bowl. Float ice cube in center.

➤NEW YEAR'S PUNCH

Yield 30 Servings

- ❖ 46 oz juice,pineapple,1 can

- ❖ 4 c tea,brewed

- ❖ 3 c juice,apple

- ❖ 1/2 c juice,lemon

- ❖ 2 c ginger ale

In a gallon container, combine pineapple juice, tea, apple juice and lemon juice; mix well. Store in refrigerator. Add the ginger ale just before serving.

➤NON ALCOHOL HOLIDAY PUNCH

Yield 30 Servings

- ❖ 6 oz frozen lemonade conc,thawed
- ❖ 6 oz frozen oj conc,thawed
- ❖ 6 c water
- ❖ 1/2 c grenadine syrup
- ❖ 1 qt ginger ale,chilled

Combine first four ingredients in a punch bowl. Just before serving, add ice cubes and gently stir in ginger ale. Put lemon slice and a cherry in each punch cup, and serve.

➤NON ALCOHOLIC TROPICAL PUNCH

Yield 1 Servings

- ❖ 6 oz strawberry gelatin
- ❖ 1 1/2 c sugar
- ❖ 2 c water,Boiling
- ❖ 1 c cold water
- ❖ 46 oz pineapple juice
- ❖ 46 oz orange juice
- ❖ 1 c lemon juice
- ❖ 1/2 ga orange sherbet
- ❖ 33 3/4 oz cold ginger ale

In two separate containers, freeze 16 ounces of orange juice and 16 ounces of pineapple juices (note you can freeze a mixture of the two juices together in a mold for decorative purposes). In a punch bowl dissolve the gelatin and the sugar with the boiling water. Add cold water and the rest of the ingredients. When ready to serve, add soft sherbet, frozen juices and cold ginger ale. Stir well.

➤NON-ALCOHOLIC FRUIT PUNCH MULL

Yield 4 Servings

- ❖ 4 c apple juice

- ❖ 1/2 c cranberry juice

- ❖ 1/2 c pineapple juice

- ❖ 1 lemon,juiced

- ❖ 1 lime,juiced

- ❖ 3 T brown sugar

- ❖ 6 cloves

- ❖ 1 cinnamon stick

- ❖ 1 orange and/or lemon,Slices
  For Garnish

Mix all ingredients together except the citrus slices and heat slowly, stirring until the sugar has dissolved. Remove from heat, leave for a few hours to infuse.

To serve, bring back to a simmer; remove and discard cloves and cinnamon. Serve in warm glasses garnished with orange and lemon slices.

Makes about 4 servings.

➤NON-ALCOHOLIC PUNCH

Yield 1 Servings

- ❖ A
- ❖ 3 lg very ripe bananas
- ❖ 2 c sugar
- ❖ 2 c water
- ❖ B
- ❖ 1/2 c orange juice
- ❖ 1cn (large) pinepple juice
- ❖ 2 bottles (or 5 tins ginger ale)

Buzz the above "A" in a blender - it looks like glop! Then add "B".

Stir into the banana/sugar/water mixture and throw in lots of ice. This is a big hit wherever it's served. It's great for a family picnic - can be served without alcohol but if adults want a little booze, add rum, rye, gin, or vodka.

45

➤OLD-FASHIONED FRUIT PUNCH

Yield 50 Servings

- ❖ 4 c tea,cold

- ❖ 4 c orange juice

- ❖ 4 lemons,juice of

- ❖ 4 oranges,thinly sliced

- ❖ 2 c sugar,to taste

- ❖ 12 c ginger ale

- ❖ 4 c soda water,or sparkling war ,Cracked

- ❖ 1 bn mint,fresh

Combine tea, juices, orange slices and sugar. Stir until the sugar dissolves. Chill. Add ginger ale and soda just before serving. Garnish with fresh mint.

SERVES about 50

➤ONE GALLON PUNCH

Yield 1 Servings

- ❖ TEA
- ❖ 4 t tea,heaping water
- ❖ SUGAR SYRUP
- ❖ 2 c sugar
- ❖ 1 c water
- ❖ REMAINING INGREDIENTS
- ❖ 1 c lemon juice
- ❖ 1 bottle ocean spray cranberry juice
- ❖ 1 sm can pineapple juice

Make a quart of hot tea. Make sugar syrup by combining sugar and water; bring to a boil and boil 5 mins. Add the tea, let cool a little. Add lemon juice, cranberry juice, and pineapple juice. Let stand until cool enough to put in frig. I put 2 trays of ice cubes in a gallon jug and then pour in the punch, add enough water to fill.

➤OPEN HOUSE PUNCH

Yield 1 Servings

- ❖ 1 fifth southern comfort

- ❖ 6 oz fresh lemon juice

- ❖ 3 qt 7-up

- ❖ 1 cn (6-oz) orange juice,Frozen

- ❖ 1 cn (6-oz) lemonade,Frozen

Chill ingredients. Mix in punch bowl, adding 7-Up just before serving.

➤ORANGE BLOSSOM PUNCH

Yield 12 Servings

- ❖ 1 c orange juice,Frozen
  -concentrate,thawed

- ❖ 10 oz strawberry daiquiri,Frozen
  -mix conc,or peach, thawed

- ❖ 750 ml champagne,see notes, chilled

- ❖ ice cubes

NOTES May use sparkling white grape juice in place of champagne. In a punch bowl combine thawed concentrates. Add 4 cups cold water; stir to combine. Gently add champagne or grape juice, but do not stir. Serve immediately over ice. If desired, garnish with strawberries and Flordia orange wedges.

➤ORANGE EGGNOG PUNCH

Yield 1 Servings

- ❖ 1 qt sherbet (raspberry,orange or lime)

- ❖ 2 c orange juice

- ❖ 2 c pineapple juice

- ❖ 1 qt dairy eggnog

- ❖ 1 c sherbet

In a mixing bowl, beat the sherbet until smooth. Add orange and pineapple juices and blend thoroughly. Gradually add the eggnog. Pour into a punch bowl. Float small scoops of sherbet on the top.

➤ORANGE PUCKS PUNCH

Yield 20 Servings

- ❖ 16 oz Orange Juice,Frozen -Concentrate

- ❖ 16 oz Lemonade Concentrate,Frozen

- ❖ 2 l Vernors Ginger Ale

- ❖ 2 l Crush

- ❖ 1 qt Orange Sherbet

- ❖ Orange (large),Slices

Mix first four ingredients. Scoop orange sherbet on top. Garnish with orange slices.

51

➤ORANGE PUNCH

Yield 1 Servings

- ❖ 1 ga tang orange drink

- ❖ 2 qt ginger ale

- ❖ 46 oz juice

Combine all ingredients in punch bowl. Add ice.

➤ORANGE SHERBET PUNCH

Yield 12 Servings

- ❖ 4 c chilled orange juice
- ❖ 1 c milk
- ❖ 3 T sugar
- ❖ 2 t orange peel,Grated
- ❖ 1/2 t nutmeg,Ground
- ❖ 1 c chilled sparkling water
- ❖ 1 qt orange sherbet

Combine 4 cups orange juice, 1 cup milk, 3 tablespoons sugar, orange peel and nutmeg in large pitcher. Mix until sugar dissolves. (Can be prepared 3 days ahead. Cover and refrigerate.)

Pour sparkling water into orange juice mixture and stir to blend. Scoop sherbet into large glass punch bowl. Pour punch over and serve immediately.

53

➤PACIFIC FRUIT PUNCH

Yield 4 Servings

- ❖ 1 lg can orange juice

- ❖ 1 lg can apricot nectar

- ❖ 1 lg can pineapple juice

- ❖ 1 qt ginger ale

- ❖ 1 c fresh strawberries

- ❖ 1 qt orange sherbet,soften in refrigerator

Combine juices and ginger ale in punchbowl. Add sherbet, strawberries, and ice. Garnish individual glass with pineapple spears and small umbrellas. Yield 4

➤PADRE PUNCH

Yield 8 Servings

- ❖ 6 oz can orange juice,Frozen -partially,Thawed

- ❖ 3orange juice cans water

- ❖ 1 qt apple cider

- ❖ 5whole cloves

- ❖ 2 cinnamon sticks

- ❖ 1 t nutmeg,Ground

- ❖ 3/4 t ginger,Ground

- ❖ Orange,Slices

In slow-cooking pot, combine orange juice with water, cider, cloves, cinnamon, nutmeg and ginger. Cover and heat on low for 4 to 6 hours (or longer). Garnish with orange slices. Keep hot and serve punch in slow-cooking pot. Recipe may be doubled if your slow-cooking pot is large enough.

55

➤PALI PUNCH

Yield 1 Servings

- ❖ 2 cn guava juice

- ❖ 1 1/2 c unsweetened pineapple juice

- ❖ 1 c fresh orange juice

- ❖ 3/4 c fresh lemon juice

- ❖ 1/4 c sugar

- ❖ 1 T grenadine syrup

- ❖ 1bottle chilled gingerale

1fresh fruit,For Garnish Combine and stir until sugar dissolves.

➤PARADISE PUNCH

Yield 1 Servings

- ❖ 16 lg oranges
- ❖ 16 lg lemons
- ❖ 2 cn (46 oz.) unsweetened pineapple juice
- ❖ 2 c sugar
- ❖ 2 c water
- ❖ 6 bottles (29 oz.) gingerale
- ❖ 1 bn mint leaves
- ❖ 1 pt fresh (or strawberries) -Frozen
- ❖ 1fresh flowers to float

Grate the rinds of 3 oranges and 3 lemons; squeeze juice from all the oranges and lemons and add the grated rinds and pineapple juice. Mix the sugar and water in a saucepan and bring to a boil, stirring until sugar is dissolved. Coll and add to juices. Add gingerale, ice, mint, berries, and flowers. Makes one full punch bowl.

57

➤PARK PLACE PUNCH

Yield 1 Servings

- ❖ 3/4 c raspberry-cranberry drink

- ❖ 2 T orange juice

- ❖ 1 t lime juice

- ❖ 1club soda

Pour raspberry-cranberry drink, orange juice and lime juice in a tall glass filled with ice. Top with club soda.

➤PARTY MILK PUNCH

Yield 12 Servings

- ❖ 1/4 c superfine sugar

- ❖ 500 ml bourbon,rye or blended whiskey

- ❖ 3 1/2 qt milk,ice cold

- ❖ 1/4 t nutmeg

Combine all except nutmeg in punch bowl. Add large block of ice and sprinkle with nutmeg.

➤PARTY PUNCH

Yield 12 Servings

- ❖ 1 c Strawberries
- ❖ 1 Apple
- ❖ 1 Orange
- ❖ 6 oz Orange Juice,Frozen
  -Concentrate,thawed
- ❖ 1 Juice Can Water
- ❖ 1 qt Orange Sherbert
- ❖ 1 qt Ginger Ale

Wash strawberries and remove stems and put into a large punch bowl. Wash apple. Carefully cut apple, lengthwise, into 4 equal pieces, cutting away the apple's core. Cut each apple quarter into 3 pieces. Place in punch bowl.

Wash and slice orange. Put orange slices in bowl. Add orange juice and water to bowl. Stir well. Spoon sherbert into bowl. Pour in ginger ale. Stir lightly and serve.

Serves 12.

➤PASSION "CHAMPAGNE" PUNCH

Yield 1 Servings

- ❖ 4 c cold diet 7-up

- ❖ 4 c cold water

- ❖ 1tub crystal light passion
  -fruit-pineapple

- ❖ 1,punch mix

In a large pitcher, combine Diet 7-UP and water. Add dry punch mix. Mix well with long-handled spoon until dissolved. Serve at once or refrigerate until ready to use.

➤PATRIDGEBERRY PUNCH

Yield 8 Servings

- ❖ 1 qt partridgeberries

- ❖ 3 T lemon juice

- ❖ 1 c orange juice

- ❖ 2 c sugar

- ❖ 6 c water

- ❖ 1 qt ginger ale

Cook partridgeberries in 4 cups of water until soft.Crush and drain through a cheese cloth.Boil sugar and remaining 2 cups of water for 5 Min.Add to Partridgeberry juice and chill.Add fruit juices.Before serving add ginger ale.

➤PAVILION PUNCH

Yield 1 Servings

- ❖ 30 ml pineapple juice,Canned
- ❖ 30 ml mango juice,Canned
- ❖ 30 ml orange juice,Canned
- ❖ a dash of rose syrup
- ❖ 15 ml fresh cream,beaten
- ❖ 10 ml soda
- ❖ 4 ice cubes
- ❖ TO GARNISH
- ❖ 1 sl pineapple
- ❖ 1 sl sweet lime
- ❖ 1cherry

PUT the ice cubes in a Chinese tumbler glass. Add pineapple juice, mango juice and orange juice to the glass. Add rose syrup and stir gently. Float with cream and top it with soda.

Serve garnished with pineapple slice, sweet lime and cherry.

➤PEACH CHAMPAGNE PUNCH

Yield 1 Servings

- ❖ 5ripe peaches,peeled, pitted,and sliced

- ❖ 2 c water

- ❖ 2 c sugar

- ❖ 1bottle of chilled champagne

In a small saucepan combine the peaches, water, and sugar, stir until sugar is dissolved, and bring to a boil. Reduce the heat and simmer for 10 minutes. Remove from the heat and allow to cool completely. Transfer mixture to a bowl and using an immersion blender or transfer mixture to a blender, puree until very smooth. Place in the refrigerator and chill for 1 hour. When ready to serve , place 2 tablespoons of the peach puree in a champagne glass and top with your favorite chilled champagne. Yield 1 quart of punch

➤ PEACHY POWER PUNCH

Yield 1 Servings

- ❖ 1/2 c ruby red grapefruit juice

- ❖ 1 peach,peeled, pitted and quartered

- ❖ ½ banana

- ❖ 1/2 c vanilla yogurt

- ❖ 2 T honey

- ❖ 1/2 c low-fat milk

- ❖ 1 wheat germ

  In a blender, puree all ingredients except milk and wheat germ until smooth (approximately 30 seconds). Add milk and process until thoroughly mixed.
  Pour into individual glasses. Sprinkle each serving with wheat germ.

➤PEPPERMINT PUNCH

Yield 8 Servings

- ❖ 4 c milk

- ❖ 2 c vanilla ice cream,softened

- ❖ 2 c chocolate ice cream,softened

- ❖ 1 peppermint extract

- ❖ 8 small candy canes

In large bowl, whisk together milk, vanilla and chocolate ice creams, and a few drops peppermint extract to taste.

Refrigerate until ready to serve. Just before serving, whisk to blend. Pour into glasses and garnish with candy canes. Makes 8 cups.

➤PEPPERMINT STICK PUNCH

Yield 1 Servings

- ❖ 1 1/2 c sugar

- ❖ 11/2 c lime juice from

- ❖ concentrate 1 c vodka (or water)

- ❖ 2 T white creme de menthe or teaspoon peppermint extra

- ❖ 2bottles (32-ounce)

- ❖ Club soda,chilled

- ❖ 1candy canes

In punch bowl, combine all ingredients except club soda and candy canes; stir until sugar dissolves. Just before serving, add club soda. Hang candy canes on edge of punch bowl or place in each punch cup for stirrer.

➤PERCOLATOR PUNCH

Yield 1 Servings

- ❖ 1 1/2 c pineapple juice
- ❖ 1 3/4 c water
- ❖ 2 c cranberry juice
- ❖ 1 T whole cloves
- ❖ 1/2 T allspice,whole
- ❖ 2 sticks cinnamon
- ❖ 1/2 t salt
- ❖ 1/2 c brown sugar

Put pineapple juice, water and cranberry juice in bottom of 8 cup percolator. Put rest of ingredients in top of percolator (basket). Perk 10 minutes. Serve hot.

➤PERKY PARTY PUNCH

Yield 40 Servings

- ❖ 2 cn (large) orange juice,Frozen

- ❖ 2cn (small) lemonade,Frozen

- ❖ 1cn pineapple juice

- ❖ 2qt ginger ale

- ❖ 1packet kool-ade (any color desired,for the punch)

- ❖ 1sugar,To Taste

- ❖ 1ice

Reconstitute orange juice and lemonade. Add pineapple juice and Kool- Aid. Mix. Sweeten to taste. Just before serving add ginger ale and ice. Makes 40 cups.

➤PERSIMMON PUNCH

- {Soo Jeung Kwa}

- ❖ 1 ga cold water

- ❖ 1/4 lb fresh ginger,rinsed, and sliced thin with,Skin On

- ❖ 1 oz cinnamon sticks - (8 to 10)

- ❖ 2c sugar,or to taste

- ❖ 6 semi-dried whole persimmons - cut 1" triangles

Bring the water to a boil with the ginger and cinnamon sticks. Cook over moderate heat for 1/2 hour. Strain the liquid and discard the ginger but leave the cinnamon in the punch.

Add the sugar while the liquid is still hot, to dissolve it. Add the persimmons to the lukewarm liquid and cool. The color of the punch becomes an old rose shade. Refrigerate the punch and serve cold.

Serve whenever wanted with any Asian food. This recipe yields 1 gallon.

➤ PINA COLADA PUNCH

Yield 30 Servings

- ❖ 5 piece ginger root,Dried bruised with spoon
- ❖ 5 T light-brown sugar
- ❖ 5 T cassia bark,broken in small pieces
- ❖ 3 1/3 c water
- ❖ 10 china teabags
- ❖ 11/3 coconut,Shredded
- ❖ 1/4 c water,Boiling
- ❖ 8 3/4 c pineapple juice
- ❖ 3 1/3 c light rum (or gin)
- ❖ 1 ice,Crushed
- ❖ 1maraschino cherries
- ❖ 1fresh pineapple chunks
- ❖ 1fresh pineapple leaves (opt)

Put ginger, sugar and cassia bark in a saucepan. Add 2/3 cup water and bring to a boil. Cover and simmer 5 minutes.

Remove from heat and add teabags. Let stand 5 minutes, then strain into a bowl. In a blender or food processor, blend coconut and boiling water 1 minute. Let stand 5 minutes, then strain into tea mixture, pressing coconut to extract all moisture.

Add pineapple juice and chill 1 hour. Add run or gin and stir well. Serve over crushed ice in tall glasses. Thread cocktail sticks with cherries and pineapple. Add a cocktail stick and swizzle stick to each glass. Garnish with pineapple leaves, if desired.

VARIATION Add more rum or gin for a stronger flavored drink.

➤PINEAPPLE CITRUS PUNCH

Yield 26 Servings

- ❖ 1 46 oz can pineapple juice

- ❖ 2 qt apple juice

- ❖ 2 l lemon-lime soft drink

- ❖ 2 6 oz can lemonade,Frozen
  -concentrate,thawed

- ❖ 2 orange,sliced

- ❖ 2 lime,sliced

Stir together first 4 ingredients. Add orange and lime slices. Serve over ice.

73

➤PINEAPPLE ICE CREAM PUNCH

Yield 1 Servings

- ❖ 1 pt Vanilla ice cream

- ❖ 1 pt Pineapple sherbet

- ❖ 1 qt Pineapple juice,chilled

- ❖ 1 qt Ginger ale,chilled

Creamy, sweet, and smooth. For very special occasions. Combine in punch bowl. Stir to break up ice cream and sherbet.

➤PINEAPPLE MINT PUNCH

Yield 35 Servings

- ❖ 1 qt sweet cider
- ❖ 2 qt gingerale
- ❖ 1 cn pineapple juice,(46 oz)
- ❖ 1 cn limeade,Frozen
- ❖ 1 orange,sliced thin
- ❖ 1 lemon,sliced thin
- ❖ 3 sprigs mint,Crushed

Mix cider, pineapple juice and limeade together. Add sliced orange, sliced lemon and crushed mint. Add gingerale just before serving.

75

➤PINEAPPLE ORANGE PUNCH

Yield 1 Servings

- ❖ 2 c unsweetened pineapple juice
- ❖ 2 c orange juice
- ❖ 1/4 c lemon juice
- ❖ 1 pt any flavor sherbet
- ❖ 1 fresh mint sprigs

Mix the juices. Divide the sherbet into six tall glasses, add the juices and stir slightly. Garnish with mint.

➤PINEAPPLE PARTY PUNCH

Yield 24 Servings

- ❖ 1 cn (46-oz) pineapple juice chilled

- ❖ 1 pt orange sherbet,softened

- ❖ 1 pt vanilla ice cream,softened

- ❖ 1 bottle (32-oz) ginger ale -chilled

Put juice, sherbet and ice cream into a large mixing bowl. Beat with mixer until blended. Pour into punch bowl and slowly add ginger ale. Makes 3 quarts.

➤PINEAPPLE PUNCH

Yield 1 Servings

- ❖ 1 lg pineapple

- ❖ 1 bananas

- ❖ 225 g strawberries,hulled (8 oz)

- ❖ 600 ml tropical fruit juice

Cut the lid off the pineapple and keep to one side. Cut the centre out of the pineapple and chop the flesh. Put in a bowl. Chop all the other fruit and add to the bowl. Add the juice.

Using a blender whiz the fruit until smooth. Pour into the pineapple or glasses and serve.

➤PINEAPPLE-LIME PUNCH

Yield 35 Servings

- ❖ 3 qt unsweetened pineapple juice
- ❖ 8 lemons, juice of
- ❖ 8 oranges, juice of
- ❖ 3 limes, juice of
- ❖ 2 c sugar
- ❖ 4 qt ginger ale
- ❖ 2 qt plain soda water
- ❖ 1 green food coloring -(optional)

Combine fruit juices and sugar. Chill thoroughly. Just before serving, add ginger ale and soda water. Tint a delicate green, if you wish.

Yield 35 cups.

➤PINEAPPLE-ORANGE PUNCH

Yield 1 Servings

- ❖ 12 oz orange-pineapple,Frozen
  -juice concentrate

- ❖ 1 water

- ❖ 3 c ginger ale

Prepare juice, adding water, according to directions on can. Just before serving add two of the juice cans (3 cups) of ginger ale.

➤ PINEAPPLE-RASPBERRY CREAM PUNCH

Yield 12 Servings

- ❖ 1 qt pineapple juice

- ❖ 2l ginger ale

- ❖ 1qt vanilla ice cream

- ❖ 1 qt raspberry sherbert

Pour pineapple juice and ginger ale over ice cream and sherbert. Stir until melted and blended.

➤PINK LADY PUNCH

Yield 2 Servings

- ❖ 1 pkgs. strawberry koolaid to simmer

- ❖ 2 8 oz cans orange juice,Frozen

- ❖ 3 cn water

- ❖ 2 8 oz cans lemon juice

- ❖ 3 cn water

- ❖ 2 46 oz cans pineapple and grapefruit juice

- ❖ 1 bottle maraschino cherries and juice

- ❖ 2 28 oz bottles ginger ale

Make up Koolaid according to package directions and heat to simmer.. All fruit juices and koolaid are to be mixed together 4 hours before serving. Add Ginger Ale just before serving.

➤PINK PASTEL PUNCH

Yield 1 Servings

- ❖ 2 pt raspberry sherbet
- ❖ 1 (12 oz.) can pink lemonade
- ❖ 4 c water
- ❖ 1 liter bottle lemon lime soda or
- ❖ 1 ginger ale
- ❖ 10 oz pkg. raspberries,Frozen thawed

Soften sherbet and lemonade and combine with water. Stir in thawed raspberries. Add lemon lime soda or ginger ale at last minute. Nice for weddings.

➤PINK PUNCH

Yield 10 Servings

- ❖ 1 pt lemon sherbert

- ❖ 2c pineapple juice,canned

- ❖ 1 pt cranberry juice cocktail

- ❖ 1 qt ginger ale

Put sherbert by spoonfuls into punch bowl. Add juices. Add ginger ale.

➤PLANTATION COFFEE PUNCH

Yield 12 Servings

- ❖ 1/4 c sugar

- ❖ 1/3 c coffee,Instant

- ❖ 1 ds salt

- ❖ 1t vanilla

- ❖ 5c milk

- ❖ 1pt vanilla (or coffee ice cream)

Whipped cream Nutmeg

Combine sugar, coffee, salt, vanilla, and milk; stir until sugar dissolves. Chill until serving time. Then ladle ice cream, by large spoonfuls, into punch bowl; pour coffee mixture over. Top with puffs of whipped cream and sprinkle with a little nutmeg. Serve in punch cups. Makes 12 servings.

➤PLANTATION PUNCH

Yield 1 Servings

- ❖ 1/4 c dark rum

- ❖ 1/4 c orange juice

- ❖ 1 T pineapple juice

- ❖ 1 T amaretto

- ❖ ice, Crushed

- ❖ orange rind, optional

Combine liquids in serving glass. Add ice to fill glass. Transfer to cocktail shaker; shake. Pour into glass. Garnish and serve.

Serves 1.

➤ PLANTER'S PUNCH - BAHAMAS STYLE

Yield 1 Servings

- ❖ 1 T lemon juice

- ❖ 1T orange juice

- ❖ 1T pineapple juice

- ❖ 1/2 T grenadine

- ❖ 1 T rum

- ❖ 1 ice, Shaved

Shake all ingredients together vigorously.

➤PLANTER'S PUNCH - JAMAICA STYLE

Yield 1 Servings

- ❖ 1 part fresh lime (or lemon) juice

- ❖ 2 parts sugar

- ❖ 3 parts dark rum

- ❖ 4 parts ice,Crushed

- ❖ 1 ds angostura bitters

- ❖ 1 maraschino cherries to decorate

Shake lime juice, sugar, rum, ice and bitters vigorously, pour into tall glasses and garnish each with a cherry.

➤PLANTER'S PUNCH

Yield 1 Servings

- ❖ 1 oz dark rum
- ❖ 1/2 oz grenadine
- ❖ 2 oz orange juice
- ❖ 1 T fresh lemon juice
- ❖ 1 t powdered sugar
- ❖ 3 oz club soda
- ❖ ice,Cracked
- ❖ ice cubes
- ❖ 1 maraschino cherry
- ❖ 1 orange slice

Fill a mixing glass with cracked ice. Add rum, grenadine, orange juice, lemon juice, and sugar. Shake and strain into collins glass filled with ice cubes. Fill with club soda. Garnish with a cherry and orange slice.

➤PONCHE DE FRUTAS (FRUIT PUNCH)

Yield 4 Servings

- ❖ 3 Oranges,juiced
- ❖ 3 Lemons,juiced
- ❖ 2 Apples,peeled, cored,
- ❖ ½ Pineapple,peeled, cored,
- ❖ 1/2 c Sugar,or to taste
- ❖ 1/2 lb Grapes
- ❖ 1/2 lb Plums,pitted
- ❖ 1 qt Strong tea,chilled
- ❖ 1 qt ice,Crushed
- ❖ 1 qt Soda water,optional

In a bowl, combine orange juice, lemon juice, apples and pineapple. Sprinkle with sugar and stir to combine. Place grapes and plums in a blender with a small amount of water and blend until pureed. Strain puree and add to bowl of sweetened fruit and stir to combine.

Place fruit mixture in a large bowl and add strong tea, crushed ice and soda water, if desired.

This recipe yields 4 to 6 servings.

➤PONCHE DE PINA (HOT PINEAPPLE PUNCH)

Yield 8 Servings

- ❖ 3 pineapples
- ❖ 3 c water
- ❖ 3 sticks cinnamon
- ❖ 2 t whole cloves
- ❖ 2 t whole allspice
- ❖ 3/4 c sugar
- ❖ 1 c coconut milk
- ❖ 1 qt light rum

Peel pineapples; chop or shred. Add water and let stand overnight. Put in large saucepan with spices, sugar, and coconut milk. Boil for 5 minutes.

Strain liquid into large pitcher. Add rum and serve hot. Makes 8-12 servings.

Note If fresh coconut milk is not available, pour sweet milk over shredded coconut. Let stand for several hours. Squeeze through a cloth.

➤PORT PUNCH

Yield 1 Servings

- ❖ 1 ga Cranberry Juice

- ❖ 2Fifths White Port

- ❖ 2 Oranges,thinly sliced

Chill cranberry juice and port, then combine in a punch bowl. Float oranges on top and serve over ice.

➤PORTOFINO PUNCH

Yield 16 Servings

- ❖ 92 oz hawaiian punch,chilled

- ❖ 2/3 c pineapple juice

- ❖ 6 oz lemonade,frozen
  concentrate,thawe

- ❖ 12 oz club soda,chilled

Combine punch, juice and lemonade in punch bowl. Just before serving, add club soda. Garnish with lemon and lime slices or fresh mint, if desired.

➤POWER PUNCH

Yield 40 Servings

- ❖ 1 fifth of whiskey
- ❖ 1 fifth of sauterne
- ❖ 1 fifth of brandy
- ❖ 1 fifth of sherry
- ❖ 1 fifth of champagne
- ❖ 1 fifth of soda water
- ❖ 1 oranges
- ❖ 1 lemons

1. Mix and chill the first four ingredients overnight.

2. At serving time, add chilled champagne and soda water.

3. Stir. Into each glass place a slice of orange and slice of lemon.

Makes 40 (4-ounce) servings.

➤PRESBYTERIAN PUNCH

Yield 8 Servings

- ❖ 32 z chilled mango juice

- ❖ 3 limes,juiced and with zest

- ❖ 4 dried habanero's,crushed

Allow to mix for 2 hours before serving.

➤PRESS CONFERENCE PUNCH

Yield 96 Servings

- ❖ 92 oz Hawaiin Punch,or Hi

- ❖ C –2 -cans

- ❖ 64 oz Five Alive Juice

- ❖ 12 oz mixed fruit,Frozen -unsweetened-- 1 bag

- ❖ 12 oz strawberries,Frozen -unsweetened-- 1 bag

- ❖ 1/2 ga sherbet,rainbow or other

- ❖ 1 ga ginger ale,

- ❖ 2- two liter bottles

- ❖ or seven up vodka,to taste -- opt'l

Stir together juices and frozen fruit in a large punch bowl. (used two fairly large bowls and put half the ingredients into each bowl.) Spoon in the sherbet. (I used a mini- ice cream scoop for this.)

Slowly pour in soda shortly before serving.

➤PRETTY PARTY PUNCH

Yield 1 Servings

- ❖ 4 c cranberry-raspberry juice

- ❖ 4c orange juice

- ❖ 2c pineapple juice

- ❖ 2c seltzer (or club soda)

- ❖ 1c fresh/frozen strawberries
  -set strawberries aside

In a large pitcher or punch bowl mix together the cranberry- raspberry juice, the orange juice, the pineapple juice & seltzer. Stir in the strawberries. Add two handfuls of ice cubes of punch isn't cold enough.

➤PSEUDO-CHAMPAGNE PUNCH

Yield 10 Servings

- ❖ 1 bottles white grape juice

- ❖ 1 bottle club soda

- ❖ 56 oz (2 bottles) 7-up

Mix ingredients. Serve well chilled. Tastes like champagne!!

➤PUCK-R-UP PUNCH

Yield 20 Servings

- ❖ 12 oz Cran-raspberry Drink,Frozen ,Thawed

- ❖ 16 oz Frozen Limeade,Thawed

- ❖ 1/3 c Powdered Orange Breakfast
  -Drink Mix As Tang

- ❖ 1/3 c Sugar

- ❖ 8 c Cold Water

- ❖ 2 l Squirt

Combine above ingredients, except Squirt, in large pitcher. Stir to mix. For individual servings, mix two-thirds of juice mixture and one-third of Squirt in a glass filled with ice. Stir to blend. Garnish with orange and lime slices.

➤PUMPKIN PUNCH

Yield 6 Servings

- ❖ 1 c pumpkin,canned puree

- ❖ 1/2 c brown sugar

- ❖ 1/4 c honey

- ❖ 1 t cinnamon

- ❖ 1/2 t nutmeg

- ❖ 1/2 c orange juice

- ❖ 1 qt vanilla yogurt,Frozen

Combine ingredients in blender and whirl until smooth. Pour into carved out pumpkin to serve.

➤PUNCH

Yield 1 Servings

- ❖ 1 pk koolaid,lemon or lime
- ❖ 2 c pineapple juice
- ❖ 2 c sugar
- ❖ 1/2 ga water,plus
- ❖ 1 pt water
- ❖ 1qt ginger ale

Mix together.

Makes 1 gallon.

➤PUNCH - ORANGE OR LIME

Yield 1 Servings

- ❖ ORANGE

- ❖ 1 pk orange kool-aid

- ❖ 1 cn frozen orange juice,(12 -oz.)

- ❖ 1 qt orange sherbet

- ❖ 2l 7-up (or ginger ale)

- ❖ LIME

- ❖ 2 pk lime kool-aid

- ❖ 1frozen lemonade ,(12 oz.)

- ❖ 1 qt lime sherbet

- ❖ 2 l 7-up (or ginger ale)

Make Kool-Aid as directions on packet. Add frozen juice, undiluted.
Add sherbet, then 7-Up when ready to serve.

➤PUNCH FOR A BUNCH

Yield 12 Servings

- ❖ 6 oz pineapple-orange,Frozen concentrate

- ❖ 6 oz grapefruit juice,Frozen concentrate

- ❖ 1 qt water

- ❖ 1 qt sugar-free lemon-lime soft-drink

Combine juice concentrates and water in a gallon container. Stir well to mix. Just before serving, add soft drink.

➤QUICK CRANBERRY PUNCH

Yield 12 Servings

- ❖ 16 ounce can pink,Frozen

- ❖ -lemonade concentrate,thawe

- ❖ 1 32 ounce bott le cranberry -juice cocktail,chilled

- ❖ 2 12 ounce cans ginger ale ,chilled

Prepare lemonade as directed on can in large pitcher.

Stir in cranberry juice cocktail and enough ice to chill. Just before serving, stir in ginger ale.

12 servings (3/4 cup each).

➤QUICK FRUIT PUNCH

Yield 30 Servings

- ❖ 1 cn (46-oz) sweetened orange -juice

- ❖ 1 cn (46-oz) sweetened pineapple -juice

- ❖ 4 c ginger ale

Chill thoroughly. Mix well. Add ginger ale last. Yield 30 servings.

➤RADIOACTIVE PUNCH

Yield 1 Servings

❖ 1 see below

Easiest is to mix something yellow with something blue. Orange juice and Mountain Dew are good for the yellow, Great Bluedini kool-aid is good for the blue. You'll end up with a radioactive shade of green.

➤RAINBOW PUNCH

Yield 6 Servings

- ❖ 3 c chilled red fruit punch drink,

- ❖ 1 qt lemon sherbet,

- ❖ 3 c chilled lemon-lime soda or sparkling water

Start with 6 tall juice glasses. Pour 1/2 cup juice into each glass. Place about 2/3cups sherbet in each glass. Fill rest of glass with soda. Serve.

➤RASPBERRY CHAMPAGNE PUNCH (BORDEN)

Yield 3 Servings

- ❖ 20 oz red raspberries in,Frozen -syrup,thawed

- ❖ 1/3 c lemon juice

- ❖ 1/2 c sugar

- ❖ 750 ml rosé

- ❖ 1 qt raspberry sherbet

- ❖ 750 ml champagne,or asti spumante,- chilled

In the blender container, pure the raspberries. In a large punch bowl, combine the pured raspberries, lemon juice, sugar and wine; stir until the sugar dissolves. Just before serving, scoop the sherbet into the punch bowl; add champagne. Stir gently.

➤RASPBERRY PUNCH

Yield 1 Servings

- ❖ 1/2 ga raspberry sherbet

- ❖ 1 46 oz. can hawaiian punch

- ❖ 1 2 liter 7-up (can use diet)

Scoop sherbet into punch bowl. Add Hawaiian Punch. Just before serving, add 7-Up. Stir gently. The sherbet will dissolve slowly and keep the punch cold.

-

➤RASPBERRY SHERBET PUNCH

Yield 10 Servings

- ❖ 1/2 ga raspberry sherbert

- ❖ 2 l ginger ale

- ❖ 33 oz pineapple juice

Combine all together and serve.

➤RECEPTION TEA PUNCH

Yield 1 Servings

- ❖ 2 qt iced tea

- ❖ 2 c cranberry cocktail juice

- ❖ 2 bottles ginger ale,(28 oz.)

- ❖ 2 cn frozen lemonade,(6 oz.)

- ❖ 2 cn frozen limeade,(6 oz.)

Pour tea into punch bowl and add lemonade, limeade and cranberry juice. Put block of ice or cubes in punch; add ginger ale just before serving.

➤RED PUNCH

Yield 1 Servings

- ❖ 1 pk cherry kool-aid
- ❖ 1pk raspberry kool-aid
- ❖ 2c sugar
- ❖ 1cn (6oz) lemonade,Frozen -concentrate
- ❖ 1cn (6oz) orange juice,Frozen -concentrate
- ❖ 3qt water
- ❖ 1 bottle,(16 oz) sprite or -7-up

Combine all ingredients except Sprite or 7-Up. Mix well. When ready to serve, add Sprite or 7-Up. Makes one gallon.

➤RED SATIN PUNCH

Yield 35 Servings

- ❖ 1 qt apple juice

- ❖ 2bottles (1-liter) 7-up

- ❖ 3 1 qt cranberry juice

- ❖ 2 trays 7-up cubes

Fill 2 ice-cube trays with 7-Up and freeze until set. Mix juices and 7-Up together and float 7-Up cubes in it.

➤RED WINE PUNCH

Yield 20 Servings

- ❖ 2 lg cans pineapple juice

- ❖ 1 lg bott cranberry juice

- ❖ 1/2 ga burgundy wine

- ❖ 1 c lemon juice

- ❖ 1 c apricot liqueur

Mix all ingredients together. Serve chilled, can be frozen. Serves 20.

➤RHUBARB CITRUS PUNCH

Yield 1 Servings

- ❖ 8 c rhubarb,Diced
- ❖ 5 c water
- ❖ 1 1/3 c sugar
- ❖ 2 c orange juice
- ❖ 3/4 c lemon juice
- ❖ 1 qt ginger ale (or 7-Up),chilled
- ❖ 1 qt fresh (or),Frozen strawberries,(optional)

In kettle, simmer rhubarb and water until rhubarb is soft. Cool; strain. Measure 4 cups juice and return to kettle with the sugar. Heat to dissolve sugar. Chill. Add the orange and lemon juices. Just before serving, add ginger ale and strawberries, if desired. Pour over ice.

➤RHUBARB PUNCH

Yield 1 Servings

- ❖ 4 c rhubarb,Cut Up
- ❖ 1/2 c sugar
- ❖ 2 c water
- ❖ 1 (6 Oz.) Can lemonade,Frozen
- ❖ 1 (12 Oz.) Can 7-Up (or white) soda

Cook until rhubarb is mushy. Strain. Add frozen lemonade. When ready to serve add the 7-Up or soda. Note Rhubarb base can be made up during rhubarb season and frozen for use with lemonade and 7-Up later.

➤ROMAN PUNCH

Yield 10 Servings

- ❖ 1 qt lemon sherbet
- ❖ 1c choice rum
- ❖ 1split of champagne,iced

In a chilled bowl, turn out the lemon sherbet. Slowly, mix the rum into it. Now quickly add the champagne which has been chilled, and serve in sherbet glasses. It should be of a mushy texture, to be drunk, not spooned.

➤ROSE PUNCH

Yield 8 Servings

- ❖ 1/2 c water
- ❖ 1/4 c sugar
- ❖ 2 c rose wine,chilled
- ❖ 1 c white grape juice,chilled
- ❖ 3 c sparkling mineral water,chilled
- ❖ 1 red (or green seedless grapes)

Heat water and sugar to boiling in small saucepan, stirring until sugar is dissolved; cool to room temperature. Mix wine, grape juice and cooled syrup in pitcher; stir in mineral water. Place small clusters of grapes in bottoms of stemmed glasses; pour punch over. Yield 8 servings (about 3/4 cup)

➤ROSE'S WEDDING PUNCH

Yield 32 Servings

- ❖ 2 lemon lime koolaid
- ❖ 3 1 1/2 c sugar
- ❖ 1 ** add water to 2 quarts
- ❖ 2 seven-up
- ❖ 1 pineapple juice
- ❖ 1/2 ga pineapple sherbert

Mix the above ingredients. Serves 32 half cups. Can add more 7-Up if you wish.

➤RUBY FRUIT PUNCH

Yield 1 Servings

- ❖ 1/4 c sugar
- ❖ 1/2 c water
- ❖ 1 (4/5 qt.) bottle rose' wine
- ❖ 2 1/2 c orange juice
- ❖ 1/4 c lemon juice
- ❖ 1 pk (10 oz.) strawberries,Frozen
- ❖ 1 (28 oz)bottle carbonated wtr
- ❖ 1 lime,Slices

In a large saucepan combine sugar and water and heat over moderately high heat tot he boiling point; then reduce heat to low and simmer 5 minutes. Remove from heat and cool. Combine wine, fruit juices, sugar syrup and strawberries. Pour over ice in a punchbowl. Stir in carbonated water when ready to serve. Garnish with lime slices.

➤RUBY PUNCH BOWL

Yield 24 Servings

- ❖ 1 1/2 c water

- ❖ 2 c sugar (or less,to taste)

- ❖ 2 3-4 inch sticks cinnamon

- ❖ 2 t whole cloves

- ❖ 1/8 t salt

- ❖ 3 bottles (750 ml) burgundy 1or other red table wine

- ❖ 2 c chilled cranberry cocktail

- ❖ 1 l chilled apple cider

- ❖ 1 ice

- ❖ 1 thin lemon (or lime),Slices

In saucepan bring water, sugar, spices and salt to boil. Lower heat and simmer 10 minutes; strain-out and discard spices; cool syrup. Combine spiced syrup with wine, cranberry juice cocktail and cider. Pour into punch bowl, add ice and lemon slices.

➤RUBY RED GRAPEFRUIT PUNCH

Yield 17 Servings

- ❖ 48 oz ruby red grapefruit juice
  -chilled

- ❖ 33 3/4 oz club soda

- ❖ 25 1/3 oz dry white wine,chilled

Combine all ingredients in a large punch bowl; stir well. Yield 17 servings (serving size 3/4 cup).

➤RUM CRANBERRY PUNCH

Yield 25 Servings

- ❖ 2 c light rum

- ❖ 1/2 c sugar

- ❖ 12 oz orange juice,Frozen concentrate

- ❖ 32 oz cranberry juice

- ❖ 28 oz ginger ale

Combine rum, sugar, orange juice and cranberry juice. Refrigerate. Just before serving, add ginger ale and ice cubes or ice ring. Makes 2-1/2 quarts.

➤RUM PUNCH

Yield 1 Servings

- ❖ 1 qt Dark Rum
- ❖ 1 qt Vodka
- ❖ 1 pt Light Rum
- ❖ 1 qt Strawberry juice
- ❖ 1 qt Orange juice
- ❖ 1 qt Pineapple juice
- ❖ 1 pt Fresh strawberries
- ❖ 1 pt Orange wedges
- ❖ 1 pt Pineapple chunks

Mix all ingredients well. Cover and chill for 24 hours.

➤RUM-LIME PUNCH

Yield 4 Servings

- ❖ 1/2 c Simple syrup

- ❖ 1 c Dark rum

- ❖ 3/4 c Fresh lime juice

- ❖ 5 T Grenadine

- ❖ 1/4 t Bitters

- ❖ 1 pn nutmeg,Ground Ice cubes

- ❖ Lime,Slices

For the simple syrup, ombine equal amounts of sugar and water, bring to a boil and cook until sugar is dissolved. Cool. Mix all punch ingredients together. Serve over ice, garnish with lime slice. This recipe yields 4 servings.

➤RYAN'S PUNCH

Yield 1 Servings

- ❖ 1 bottle absolute vodka

- ❖ 1 ga hawiian punch

- ❖ 1/2 ga pineapple juice

Mix in a large pot or bowl, refrigerate or chill with ice.

➤SANGRIA PUNCH

Yield 8 Servings

- ❖ 2/3 c lemon juice
- ❖ 1/3 c orange juice
- ❖ 1/4 c sugar
- ❖ 1 bottle (750 milliliters) dry red wine

Strain juices. Add sugar, stirring until dissolved. Mix juice mixture and wine. Add ice. Garnish each serving with twist of lemon peel if desired. .

➤SANTA'S PUNCH

Yield 1 Servings

- ❖ 1 qt pineapple juice

- ❖ 1pk (2 qt) lime kool-aid

- ❖ 1 qt lime sherbet

- ❖ 2 qt ginger ale

Preparation Mix Kool-aid in punch bowl. Add pineapple juice. Just before serving, add sherbet by spoonfuls. Add ginger ale. For red punch, use raspberry Kool-aid and sherbet.

➤SCOTTISH (ROSS'S) WHISKEY PUNCH

Yield 1 Servings

- ❖ 2 lemons
- ❖ 1 orange
- ❖ 8 oz demarara (raw brown) sugar
- ❖ 1 (4oz for a sharper punch 8 oz for a sweeter punch)
- ❖ 1 t ginger essence (extract)
- ❖ 4 cloves
- ❖ 2 cinnamon sticks
- ❖ 3 ds angostura bitters
- ❖ 1 3/4 pt water,Boiling
- ❖ 1bottle scotch whiskey
- ❖ 2 sherry glasses of green
- ❖ 1 ginger wine

Slice lemons and orange into a large bowl. Add the sugar, ginger essence, cloves, cinnamon and bitters.

Pour over the boiling water and leave to cool. When cool, add the whiskey and the green ginger wine. Cover and leave overnight. To serve, transfer to a punch bowl and top with ice, or reheat and serve warm.

➤SEA CAPTAIN'S PUNCH

Yield 1 Servings

- ❖ 1 qt strong tea

- ❖ 1lemons

- ❖ 1fifth dark rum

- ❖ 1/2 c brandy

- ❖ 1/4 c peach brandy

- ❖ 2 c unsweetened pineapple juice

Combine 1 qt. cold water and 3 teabags of tea in a large container.

Let brew either outside or in refrigerator about 1 hour. Meanwhile, remove rind from the lemon. Cut the rind into thin strips. Add the rind and juice of the lemons to the brewed tea. Cover and store overnight at room temperature.

Just before serving, pour tea mixture, rum, pineapple juice, and both brandies over a block of ice in a punch bowl.

➤SEA FOAM PUNCH

Yield 1 Servings

- ❖ 1 pk (2.5-oz) unsweetened lemon lime soft drink mix

- ❖ 1/2 c sugar

- ❖ 1 qt cold milk

- ❖ 1pt vanilla ice cream

- ❖ 2 bottles (7-oz) lemon-lime

Place soft drink powder, sugar & milk in a large punch bowl, stir to dissolve. Add ice cream by spoonfuls. Resting bottle on rim of the bowl,

**Carefully pour in carbonated beverage. Serve immediately.
Serves 15.**

➤SHERBET AND GINGER ALE PUNCH

Yield 16 Servings

- ❖ 2 l sherbet (use your favorite flavor o

- ❖ 2 l ginger ale

1. Scoop sherbet into punch bowl. Slowly pour ginger ale over the sherbet.

2. Serve.

3. Replenish sherbet and/or ginger ale as needed.

➤SHERBET CHAMPAGNE PUNCH

Yield 20 Servings

- ❖ 1 1/2 c pineapple juice,chilled

- ❖ 1 1/2 c orange juice,chilled

- ❖ 3/4 c lemon juice

- ❖ 1 qt orange sherbet

- ❖ 31/4 c champagne,chilled

- ❖ 10 strawberries,fresh,
  -optional

In punch bowl, combine pineapple, orange and lemon juices. Just before serving, scoop sherbet into punch bowl. Add champagne, stirring gently. Garnish each glass with whole strawberry, if desired.

➤SHERBET PUNCH

Yield 25 Servings

- ❖ 4 1/2 c sugar

- ❖ 3 c lemon juice

- ❖ 2 1/2 c pineapple juice

- ❖ 1 qt ginger ale (or champagne or) -white table wine

- ❖ 2 qt sherbet,(up to 3)

- ❖ 1 qt water

- ❖ 3 c orange juice

- ❖ 2 c water

Cook sugar and 1 qt. water together until sugar is dissolved. Chill. Add fruit juices, 2 cups water and chill. When ready to serve, stir in ginger ale or wine, then drop in sherbet by scoops.

137

➤SHIRLEY'S PUNCH

Yield 24 Servings

- ❖ 1 qt ice cream

- ❖ 1 ga sweet milk

- ❖ 1 bottle concentrated hawaiian punch

Combine all ingredients in a punch bowl.

➤SHOWER PUNCH

Yield 10 Servings

- ❖ 12 oz limeade,Frozen
- ❖ 1/2 l 7-up
- ❖ 1/2 ga lime sherbert
- ❖ 1/2 l good quality vodka
- ❖ 1 ice cubes

In a large punchbowl, combine the thawed limeade with the 7-Up and the Vodka. Scoop the lime sherbert in large chunks and add to the punchbowl. Add about 1 quart of ice cubes. Stir and enjoy.

➤SILVER PUNCH

Yield 20 Servings

- ❖ ¼ bottle gin

- ❖ 1 bottle champagne -- (brut)

- ❖ 28 oz club soda

- ❖ 28 oz 7-up®

Chill all ingredients well before mixing in a chilled punch bowl.

Add a large block or ring of ice (a tube pan is handy for freezing a ice ring) to keep everything cold. Serve in stem glasses (Champagne glasses are pretty for this) instead of punch cups.

➤SLEIGH RIDE PUNCH

Yield 1 Servings

- ❖ 3 qt Cranberry juice
- ❖ 1lb Tangerines,in 1/2" slices
- ❖ 1/2 t cloves,Ground
- ❖ 4 Cinnamon sticks 1
- ❖ qt Sprite
- ❖ 1 l Captain Morgan's Spiced Rum Festive ice mold

In a sauce pan, bring the cranberry juice, tangerines, cloves, and cinnamonsticks up to a boil. Remove the pan from the heat and set aside. This will infuse the tangerines and spices into the juice. Chill the infused juice, completely. In a punch bowl, whisk the juice, sprite and rum together. Chill the punchcompletely before serving. Serve the punch in a pretty punch bowl with andfestive ice mold.

This recipe yields 1 gallon of punch.

➤SLUSH WITH A PUNCH

Yield 1 Servings

- ❖ 3/4 c sugar

- ❖ 7 c water

- ❖ 12 oz can lemonade,Frozen

- ❖ 1 concentrate,thawed &
  1undiluted

- ❖ 12 oz can orange juice,Frozen

- ❖ 1 concentrate,thawed &
  1 undiluted

- ❖ 6 oz can pineapple juice,Frozen

- ❖ 1 concentrate,thawed &
  1undiluted

- ❖ 1 to 1/2 cup coconut liqueur

- ❖ 5 to 6 cups lemon-lime

- ❖ 1 carbonated beverage

❖ 1 chilled

Combine sugar & water in a saucepan; bring to boil, stirring until sugar dissolves. Cool. Add concentrates & liqueur, stirring well. Pour mix into large freezer-safe container, & freeze. To serve, spoon about 1 cup slush mixture into a glass & add 1/2 cup lemon-lime beverage, stirring until slushy.

➤SLUSHY WEDDING PUNCH

Yield 100 Servings

- ❖ 10 cn (12 oz. ea.) lemonade,Frozen concentrate, thawed

- ❖ 10 cn (12 oz. ea.) orange,Frozen juice concentrate, thawed

- ❖ 20 cn (12 oz. ea.) water

- ❖ 12 oz apricot nectar

- ❖ 2 boxes (10 oz. ea.),Frozen strawberries or raspberries

- ❖ 8 bottles (1 liter ea.)

- ❖ -lemon-lime ca,rbonated bev

In a large container such as a plastic jug (or several), mix lemonade, orange juice, waer, nectar and strawberries. Freeze 2-3 hours before serving. Just before serving, chop up partially-frozen mixture in a punch bowl. Add carbonated beverage.

Makes 100-125 servings.

➤SNOW PUNCH

Yield 6 Servings

- ❖ 3 ripe bananas

- ❖ 1 c light cream

- ❖ 1/2 c sugar

- ❖ 3 7-oz bottles lemon-lime soda chilled

- ❖ 1 c lemon sherbet

- ❖ 3 T flaked coconut

Advance preparation Pour lemon juice into blender container. Slice bananas into container. Cover; blend till pureed. Combine banana mixture, cream, and sugar; chill. Before serving Add lemon-lime soda, stirring gently to blend. Serve in small glasses or punch cups. Top with spoonfuls of lemon sherbet; sprinkle with flaked coconut.

➤SOO JEUNG KWA (PERSIMMON PUNCH)

Yield 1 Servings

- ❖ 1 ga ,water, cold

- ❖ 1/4 lb ginger,fresh,rinsed, sliced thin with

- ❖ 1 oz cinnamon sticks,8-10 2 c sugar,or to taste

- ❖ 6 whole semi-dried persimmons - cut into 1 triangles

1. Bring the water to a boil with the ginger and cinnamon sticks. Cook over moderate heat for 1/2 hour. Strain the liquid and discard the ginger but leave the cinnamon in the punch.

2. Add the sugar while the liquid is still hot, to dissolve it. Add the persimmons to the lukewarm liquid and cool. The color of the punch becomes an old rose shade. Refrigerate the punch and serve cold. Serve whenever wanted with any Asian food. Makes 1 gallon.

➤SOUTH PACIFIC ISLANDS RUM PUNCH

Yield 1 Servings

- ❖ 12 bottles light rum
- ❖ 12bottles dark rum
- ❖ 2lb raw (or dark brown sugar)
- ❖ 5whole vanilla beans
- ❖ 6 dozen oranges
- ❖ 6 dozen lemons
- ❖ 6 limes
- ❖ 6 lg grapefruit
- ❖ 10 ripe bananas
- ❖ 2 ripe pineapples
- ❖ 6 bottles dry white wine -chilled
- ❖ 15 + gallon container (see -notes)
- ❖ orange,lemon and lime -slices for decoration

Pours rums into container. Add sugar and vanilla beans. Stir until sugar is dissolved. Cut the citrus fruits in half. Squeeze juice into the rum; then toss in the shells. Peel and slice the bananas.

Peel and slice the pineapple.

Add banana and pineapple to rum. Cover container and let stand in a cool place for two to three days. Stir several times during each day.

On the day of the celebration, remove pulp, vanilla beans and citrus rinds. Pour rum mixture over ice in a large punch bowl and let chill for a few hours. Just before serving add chilled white wine. Decorate bowl with sliced citrus fruits and float a few slices in the punch. If you don't have a large punch bowl, add ice to the container; let chill. Add wine just before serving - float citrus slices in the punch.

125 to 150 servings

➤SOUTHERN COMFORT PUNCH

Yield 12 Servings

- ❖ 6 md lemons
- ❖ 3md navel oranges
- ❖ 1z lemonade,Frozen
- ❖ 6oz orange juice,Frozen
- ❖ 1concentrate
- ❖ 2 l lemon-lime soda
- ❖ 1 l southern comfort

Line 2 baking sheets with plastic wrap and set aside. Slice lemons into rounds as thin as possible. Arrange lemon slices in layers on one prepared baking sheet. Repeat with oranges; layer on second baking sheet. Place in freezer for 2 to 2 1/2 hours, until fruit slices are frozen. Just before serving, open the cans of frozen lemonade and orange juice, and place frozen juices in a large punch bowl. Add the soda, Southern Comfort and several handfuls of ice.

Remove frozen fruit slices from freezer and arrange over the top of punch. Serve immediately.

➤SOUTHERN FRESH FRUIT PUNCH

Yield 18 Servings

- ❖ 6 lg lemons,up to 8
- ❖ 4 lg oranges,up to 6
- ❖ 2 qt water
- ❖ 1 1/2 c sugar
- ❖ 8 regular-size tea bags
- ❖ 1 c fresh pineapple,Diced

PEEL lemons and oranges; carefully remove and discard pith, reserving rind. SQUEEZE juice from lemons to measure 11/2 cups; squeeze juice from oranges to measure 2 cups. Set juices aside. BRING 2 quarts water and sugar to a boil in a large saucepan, stirring often; boil 1 minute. Pour over tea bags and rind; cover and steep 20 minutes. DISCARD tea bags and rind, squeezing tea bags gently.

STIR in juices and pineapple. Cover and chill at least 2 hours. Serve over ice. Yield about 3 quarts.

➤SPACE NEEDLE BLAST-OFF PUNCH

Yield 1 Servings

- ❖ 1/2 oz orgeat syrup

- ❖ 3/4 oz orange curacao

- ❖ 1 1/2 oz sweet and sour

- ❖ 1 1/2 oz orange juice

- ❖ 1 1/2 oz white rum

- ❖ 1 oz rum

- ❖ 1 garnish,stemmed maraschino

Combine all ingredients. Shake well and pour over ice in Tom Collins glass. Garnish.

152

➤SPARKLE PUNCH

Yield 1 Servings

- ❖ 1 1 1/2 liter chablis

- ❖ 1 sprite

Pour wine and soda pop over block of ice in punch bowl. Add red maraschino cherries to suit. Serve over ice cubes in tall glasses.

➤SPARKLING APPLE PUNCH

Yield 16 Servings

- ❖ 2 cinnamon sticks

- ❖ 3 64 oz apple juice

- ❖ 2 c unsweetened orange juice

- ❖ 2 (25.4 oz)bottles sparkling apple cider

- ❖ 1 icy fruit wreath

Drop cinnamon sticks into bottle of apple juice; chill atleast 2 hours. Pour juice into a large punch bowl, discarding cinnamon. Pour in orange juice and apple cider.

➤SPARKLING CHAMPAGNE PUNCH

Yield 7 Servings

- ❖ 24 z lemonade concentrate,Frozen -thawed,and undiluted
- ❖ 24z pineapple juice concentrate -thawed,and undiluted
- ❖ 6c water
- ❖ 1ice cubes (or ice ring)
- ❖ 2 33.8 oz bottles ginger ale -chilled
- ❖ 28 z tonic water,chilled
- ❖ 125.4 oz bottle champagne -chilled

Combine first 3 ingredients; chill well. To serve punch, pour juice mixture over ice in a large punch bowl. Gently stir in ginger ale, tonic water, and champagne.

Yeild 7 quarts

➤SPARKLING CRANBERRY PUNCH

Yield 25 Servings

- ❖ qt cranberry juice cocktail
  -chilled

- ❖ 6 oz pink lemonade,Frozen -concentrate,thawed

- ❖ 32 oz sparkling water,chilled

Mix cranberry juice cocktail and lemonade concentrate in punch bowl.

Just before serving, stir in sparkling water. 25 servings (about 1/2 cup each);

➤SPARKLING CRANBERRY-APRICOT PUNCH

Yield 32 Servings

- ❖ 48 oz cranberry-apricot drink

- ❖ 2 25oz bottles white grape jce

- ❖ 2 md apricots,sliced

- ❖ 2 16oz bottles soda

Chill ingredients. Mix cranberry-apricot juice and grape juice in punch bowl. Just before serving, stir in soda (sparkling water) and apricots.

➤SPARKLING FALL HARVEST PUNCH

Yield 10 Servings

- ❖ 2 c cranberry juice

- ❖ 2 c apple juice

- ❖ 1 1/2 c orange juice

- ❖ 2 c club soda

- ❖ 1 orange slices,For Garnish

- ❖ 1 cranberries,For Garnish

Combine juices in a large bowl or pitcher.

Just before serving, add club soda and stir. Garnish with sliced oranges and fresh whole cranberries.

➤SPARKLING MOCK CHAMPAGNE PUNCH

Yield 10 Servings

- ❖ 3/4 c sugar

- ❖ 1 c water

- ❖ 1 c grapefruit juice

- ❖ 1/2 c orange juice

- ❖ 1/2 c grenadine

- ❖ 1 1/2 c ginger ale,chilled

- ❖ 1 twists lemon peel,optional maraschino cherries

- ❖ -optional

In small saucepan, combine sugar and water. Simmer about 1 minute or until sugar is dissolved, stirring constantly. Pour grapefruit juice, orange juice and grenadine into 2 quart non-metal container; mix in sugar/water mixture. Refrigerate. Just before serving, pour into punch bowl; add ginger ale, pouring slowly down sides of bowl. Serve over ice. If desired, garnish with lemon peel and maraschino cherry.

➤SPARKLING PINEAPPLE PUNCH

Yield 10 Servings

- ❖ 1 c guava nectar

- ❖ 1 one,(3-pound) ripe

- ❖ 1 pineapple--peeled,

- ❖ 1,cored and cut into

- ❖ 1,1-inch chunks

- ❖ 2 1/4 c honey

- ❖ 3 qt cold unsweetened pineapple -juice,(see note)

- ❖ 1 two,(750-ml) bottles

- ❖ 1 ,cold brut sparkling

- ❖ 1 ,wine

- ❖ 3/4 c calvados (or cognac)

1. Pour the guava nectar into an 8-inch metal ring mold or
   kugelhopf mold; the nectar should cover the bottom of the

mold. Freeze until firm, about 25 minutes. Put the pineapple chunks and honey in a blender and puree until smooth. Pour the pineapple puree over the frozen guava nectar, cover and freeze until solid, at least 2 hours.

2. In a large punch bowl, combine the pineapple juice, sparkling wine and Calvados. Warm the bottom of the mold under hot water to thoroughly loosen the pineapple ice. Invert the ring onto a sheet pan, then carefully lower it into the punch, guava side up. Ladle the punch into glasses and serve.

➤SPARKLING PUNCH

Yield 10 Servings

- ❖ 6 oz grape juice,Frozen -concentrate

- ❖ 6 oz orange juice,Frozen -concentrate

- ❖ 6 oz lemonade concentrate,Frozen

- ❖ 4 c water

- ❖ 1 qt ginger ale,diet

Combine all ingredients except ginger ale; chill several hours. At serving time, slowly pour in ginger ale. Serve over cracked ice. If desired, garnish with frosted Tokay grapes. 10 to 12 servings.

➤SPARKLING RED SLUSH PUNCH

Yield 2 Servings

- ❖ 2 c sugar

- ❖ 1cn pineapple juice,large can

- ❖ 2 qt cranberry juice

Stir sugar into boiling water. Let cool. Add other liquids and freeze. Remove from freezer 1/2 hour before serving. Scoop out slush into punch bowl. When bowl is 1/2 full, slowly add lemon-lime soda (1 gallon maximum). Slush mixture with back of spoon before serving.

➤SPARKLING ROSE' PUNCH

Yield 50 Servings

- ❖ 2 pk sliced strawberries,Frozen -thawed

- ❖ 1/2 c sugar

- ❖ 2 bottles,(4/5 qt. each) rose' wine

- ❖ 2 cn (6 oz. each) lemonade concentrate

- ❖ 1qt sparkling water,well chilled

- ❖ 1ice cubes (or block of ice.)

In a bowl combine berries, sugar and 1 bottle wine. Cover and let stand for 1 hour at room temperature. Strain mixture into punch bowl. Add frozen lemonade concentrate, stir until completely thawed. Add remaining bottles of wine, pour in sparkling water. Add ice.

➤SPARKLING STRAWBERRY PUNCH

Yield 1 Servings

- ❖ 2 pk (10-oz) strawberries,Frozen ,Thawed

- ❖ 1 cn (6-oz) lemonade,Frozen slightly,Thawed

- ❖ 1 fifth rose wine,chilled

- ❖ 2 bottles (28-oz) ginger ale,chilled

- ❖ 1 bottle (28-oz) club soda -chilled

- ❖ 2 trays ice cubes

- ❖ 1/4 c sugar

- ❖ 1 sl orange,For Garnish

About 10 minutes before serving, blend strawberries & lemonade concentrate in blender. Cover & at high speed, blend until well mixed. Pour this mixture into a chilled punch bowl. Add all ingredients except orange slices. Stir punch until sugar is completely dissolved. Garnish with orange slices. Makes 18 cups.

➤SPICE PARTY PUNCH

Yield 4 Servings

- ❖ 1 cn (46 oz.) -pineapple-grapefruit juice

- ❖ 1 qt apple juice

- ❖ 3 cn (6 oz.) orange juice,Frozen concentrate

- ❖ 1 cn (5 3/4 oz.) lemon,Frozen juice

- ❖ 24 whole cloves

- ❖ 3   pieces (3 in.) cinnamon

- ❖ 1/2 t ginger

- ❖ 1/2 t allspice,Ground

- ❖ 1/2 t mace

- ❖ 1 c sugar

- ❖ 4 qt ginger ale

Combine fruit juices. Tie cloves in cheesecloth bag (unless you want to go fishing for them later); add to juices with other spices and sugar. Mix well. Let stand several hours. When ready to serve, remove spice bag; stir well. Pour over ice in punch bowl; add ginger ale.

➤SPICED APRICOT PUNCH

Yield 12 Servings

- ❖ 1 46 ounce ca apricot nectar

- ❖ 3 c orange juice

- ❖ 1/2 c brown sugar,Packed

- ❖ 2 T lemon juice

- ❖ 3 cinnamon sticks

- ❖ 1/2 t whole cloves

In slow-cooking pot, combine apricot nectar, orange juice, brown sugar, and lemon juice. Tie cinnamon and cloves in small cheesecloth bag; add to juices. Cover and heat on low for 2 to 5 hours. Serve hot from pot.

➤SPICED HOT PERCOLATOR PUNCH

Yield 16 Servings

- ❖ 1 qt apple cider

- ❖ 1 pt cranberry juice

- ❖ 1 pt orange juice

- ❖ 1/2 c sugar

- ❖ 1 t allspice,whole

- ❖ 3 cinnamon sticks

1. Combine cider and juices in automatic percolator.

2. Place sugar and spices in basket.

3. Allow it to go through cycle.

4. Serve hot.

Makes 16 servings.

➤SPICED PEACH PUNCH

Yield 12 Servings

- ❖ 1 (46 oz.) can peach nectar
- ❖ 1 (20 oz.) can orange juice
- ❖ 1/2 c brown sugar,firmly packed
- ❖ 3 (3 inch) pieces stick cinnamon,broken
- ❖ 1/2 t whole cloves
- ❖ 2 T lime juice

Combine peach nectar, orange juice, and brown sugar in a large saucepan. Tie cinnamon sticks and cloves in a cheesecloth bag and drop into saucepan.

Heat slowly, stirring constantly, until sugar dissolves; simmer 10 minutes. Stir in lime juice; ladle into mugs. You may garnish with cinnamon sticks. Serve warm. Yield 12

➤SPICED PERCOLATOR PUNCH

Yield 22 Servings

- ❖ 9 c unsweetened pineapple
- ❖ 1 juice
- ❖ 9 c cranberry juice
- ❖ 1 cocktail
- ❖ 4 1/2 c water
- ❖ 1 c brown sugar.
- ❖ 1 coffee basket
- ❖ 4 1/2 teaspoons whole cloves
- ❖ 4 cinnamon sticks,broken
- ❖ ¼ teaspoon salt

In a party-size coffee pot (24-30 cups) combine the 9 cups of unsweetened pineapple juice, 9 cups cranberry juice cocktail, 4-1/2 cups water, and 1 cup of brown sugar. In the basket assemble place the cloves, cinnamon sticks, and salt. Assemble, plug in, and perk. Serve piping hot. Makes approxomately 22 servings.

➤SPICY PERCOLATOR PUNCH

Yield 1 Servings

- ❖ 2 c cranberry juice
- ❖ 2 1/2 c pineapple juice
- ❖ 1/2 c water
- ❖ 1/3 c brown sugar,Packed
- ❖ 2 sticks cinnamon,2inch
- ❖ 1/2 t whole cloves
- ❖ 1/2 t whole allspice

Place cranberry juice, pineapple juice, water & brown sugar in percolator. Place cinnamon, cloves & allspice in basket. Perk as for coffee.

➤SPICY PERK-A-PUNCH

Yield 30 Servings

- ❖ 2 qt cranberry juice cocktail

- ❖ 2 qt pineapple juice,unsweetened

- ❖ 1 qt water

- ❖ 2/3 c brown sugar

- ❖ 1 T cloves,whole

- ❖ 1 T allspice,whole

- ❖ 4 cinnamon sticks,2 Inch

- ❖ 2 lemons,sliced, quartered

Combine juices and water in bottom of 30 cup percolator. Place remaining ingredients in filter-lined basket. Percolate 30 minutes.

➤SPICY PINEAPPLE PUNCH

Yield 4 Servings

- ❖ 225 ml water
- ❖ 500 ml pineapple juice
- ❖ 12 1/2 cm cinnamon,broken into pieces
- ❖ 6 cloves
- ❖ 6 green cardamoms,bruised
- ❖ 1 1/2 t fresh mint leaves,chopped
- ❖ -(7 g) 90 ml brandy

PUT the water, half the pineapple juice, cinnamon, cloves, cardamom and mint into a saucepan. Bring to the boil, cover the pan and simmer gently for 20 minutes.

Remove from the heat and allow to cool. Keep the pan covered. Strain the drink and add the remaining pineapple juice and the brandy. Mix well.

➤SPIRITED COFFEE PUNCH

Yield 14 Servings

- ❖ 1stephen ceideburg
- ❖ 8 c water,Boiling
- ❖ 1/3 c coffee granules,Instant
- ❖ 1/4 c granulated sugar
- ❖ 1 c kahlua (or other)
- ❖ -coffee-flavored liqueur 2 c 2-percent milk
- ❖ 1 t vanilla
- ❖ 1qt vanilla ice cream,softened
- ❖ 1whipping cream,whipped, -optional

Combine water, coffee granules and sugar, stirring until coffee dissolves; chill. Add Kahlua and milk, vanilla and ice cream, stirring until blended. Ladle beverage into cups. Top with whipped cream, if desired.

Makes 14 cups

➤SPRING BREEZE PUNCH

Yield 1 Servings

- ❖ c Cold water

- ❖ 6 oz tangerine juice - (1,Frozen
  -can),thawed

- ❖ 6 oz grapefruit juice - (1,Frozen
  - can),thawed

- ❖ qt Sparkling water

Combine all ingredients. Serve well chilled. This recipe yields 1

½ quarts of punch.

Comments Pour sparkling water into punch 1 hour or less before serving, otherwise punch will be flat.

➤SPRINGTIME PUNCH

Yield 6 Servings

- ❖ 2 c Sugar
- ❖ 2 1/2 c Water
- ❖ 1 c Fresh lemon juice (3 to 4 -lemons)
- ❖ 1 c Fresh orange juice (2 to 3 -oranges)
- ❖ 6 oz Can pineapple juice,Frozen Concentrate,thawed
- ❖ 2 qt Ginger ale,chilled

In a saucepan, bring sugar and water to a boil. Boil for 10 minutes; remove from the heat. Stir in the lemon, orange and pineapple juices. Refrigerate. Just before serving, combine ginger ale in a large punch bowl.

➤ST PADDY'S DAY PUNCH

Yield 36 Servings

- ❖ PATTI VDRJA
- ❖ 1/2 ga vanilla ice cream
- ❖ 1/2 pt whole milk
- ❖ 24 oz gingerale
- ❖ 1 peppermint -or- creme de -menthe flavoring
- ❖ 1 green food coloring

Soften ice cream in punch bowl with milk. Add peppermint flavoring to taste. At last minute, add gingerale and green food coloring.

➤ST. PATTY'S PUNCH

Yield 52 Servings

- ❖ 20 oz pineapple in juice,Crushed -chilled

- ❖ 8 dr green food color (opt)

- ❖ 18 oz lemonade concentrate,Frozen ,Thawed

- ❖ 46 oz white grape juice,chilled

- ❖ 46 oz pineapple juice,chilled

- ❖ 32 ice cubes

- ❖ 36 oz beer,chilled

Tint pineapple (with liquid) with 4 drops of the food color. Mix lemonade concentrate, juices and pineapple. Tint with remaining food color; pour on ice cubes in punch bowl. Just before serving, stir in beer. About 52 servings (1/2 cup each).

➤STARS & STRIPES PUNCH

Yield 3 Servings

- ❖ 6 oz pkg cherry gelatin
- ❖ 2 c water**,Boiling
- ❖ 2 qt chilled apple juice
- ❖ 1/2 c chilled lemon juice
- ❖ 1 1/2 qt lemon soda
- ❖ 1 ice,Cracked

Dissolve gelatin in water. Stir in fruit juices and soda; mix well. Chill with ice in punch bowl.

** DO NOT MIX HOT INGREDIENTS IN PUNCH BOWL! **

➤STEAMING HOT HOLIDAY PUNCH

Yield 20 Servings

- ❖ 3 c apple juice
- ❖ 3 c orange juice
- ❖ 6 c cranberry juice cocktail
- ❖ 3/4 c maple syrup
- ❖ 2 t powdered sugar
- ❖ 1 1/2 t cinnamon,Ground
- ❖ 3/4 t cloves,Ground
- ❖ 3/4 t nutmeg,Ground
- ❖ 1 cinnamon sticks,*see note

Combine all the ingredients in a very large heavy pan, except the cinnamon sticks. Bring to a boil and turn to simmer for few minutes. You can put the ingredients in a crockpot after it has boiled and keep warm over low heat.

➤STRAWBERRY CHAMPAGNE PUNCH

Yield 24 Servings

- ❖ 1 c water

- ❖ 1 (3 oz.) pkg. strawberry flavor gelatin

- ❖ 1 (6 oz.) can lemon,Frozen concentrate, thawed

- ❖ 2 c cold water

- ❖ 1 (750 ml) bottle rose wine -chilled

- ❖ 1 (750 ml) bottle champagne -chilled

- ❖ 1 pt (2 cups) fresh strawberries -with stems, frozen

In small saucepan, bring water to a boil. Add gelatin; stir until gelatin is dissolved. Cool.

In punch bowl, combine gelatin mixture, lemonade concentrate and cold water; mix well. Just before serving, stir in wine, champagne and frozen strawberries. Yield 24 (1/2 cup) servings.

➤STRAWBERRY DAIQURI PUNCH

Yield 1 Servings

- ❖ 1 1/2 pt strawberries,Frozen

- ❖ 1 sm can lemonade,Frozen

- ❖ 1 pt cherry sherbert

- ❖ 1 qt ginger ale

- ❖ 1 rum (optional),To Taste

Partially thaw strawberries. Put in blender or food processor; puree. Add lemonade and sherbert; blend. Put in punch bowl and add ginger ale. Top with strawberries.

➤STRAWBERRY GINGER PUNCH

Yield 20 Servings

- ❖ 1 pk (4-serving size) jello brand gelatin, strawberry

- ❖ 1/4 c sugar

- ❖ 1 1/2 c water,Boiling

- ❖ 2 1/2 c cold water

- ❖ 1 pk (10-oz) birds eye quick thaw - strawberries

- ❖ 1 cn (6-oz) concentrated,Frozen lemonade,or limeade

- ❖ 1 bottle (1-liter) ginger ale - chilled

- ❖ 1 mint leaves

- ❖ 1 ice cubes (optional)

DISSOLVE gelatin and sugar in boiling water. Add cold water, strawberries and concentrate; stir until strawberries and concentrate are thawed. Chill until ready to serve. Stir in ginger ale and mint.

Serve over ice, if desired.

MAKES 10 cups or 20 servings

➤STRAWBERRY MARGARITA PUNCH

Yield 20 Servings

- ❖ 8 cn limeade,Frozen
- ❖ 1pk strawberries,Frozen
- ❖ 1container
- ❖ 2 qt jose cuervo tequilla
- ❖ 4 c water
- ❖ 10 lb bag
- ❖ 1 fresh strawberries
- ❖ 1 ice,Crushed

Defrost Lime Aide in a large punch bowl. Add 4 c. water plus 2 qts tequilla. Blend frozen strawberries with a little of the lime/tequilla mix from the bowl, then add to the bowl. Set aside a few fresh strawberries for garnish, and puree the rest to add to the punch. Add 3/4 of the 10 lb bag of crused ice to the punch bowl. Float reserved strawberries on top.

➤STRAWBERRY PARTY PUNCH

Yield 1 Servings

- ❖ 4 pk sliced strawberries,Frozen -
  z. each) (partially),Thawed

- ❖ 1c sugar

- ❖ 2 qt rose' wine (or strawberry)
  -soda,divided

- ❖ 1 cn pink lemonade,Frozen

- ❖ -concentrate,thawed (6 oz.)

- ❖ 1 qt club soda,chilled

- ❖ Ice ring,(optional)

In large bowl, combine strawberries and sugar; mix well. Stir in 1 quart of the wine; let stand at room temperature 1 hour. Stir in concentrate; refrigerate until ready to serve. To serve, stir in remaining 1 quart wine and club soda. Serve in punch bowl with ice ring, if desired.

Yield twenty-five (1-cup) servings.

185

➤STRAWBERRY PUNCH

Yield 30 Servings

- ❖ 1 lg Lemonade Concentrate,Frozen,Thawed

- ❖ 46 oz Pineapple Juice

- ❖ 64 oz Cranberry Juice Cocktail

- ❖ 2 qt Ginger Ale

- ❖ 1 20-Oz Pkg.,Frozen
  Strawberries,(keep frozen)

Mix all ingredients together. Makes 30-40 servings.

➤STRAWBERRY SPARKLE PUNCH

Yield 1 Servings

- ❖ 4 c strawberries -- unsweetened
- ❖ 1pk strawberry jello
- ❖ 1c water --,Boiling
- ❖ 1cn lemonade,frozen concentrate
- ❖ 32 oz cranberry juice coctail
- ❖ 2 c cold water
- ❖ 28 oz ginger ale

Puree strawberries in blender; place puree in large punch bowl. Strain, if desired, to remove seeds. Dissolve gelatin in boiling water; stir in lemonade concentrate. Add mixture to punch bowl. Add cranberry cocktail and cold water. Slowly add ginger ale.

➤ STRAWBERRY-LEMONADE PUNCH

Yield 12 Servings

- ❖ 1 cn (6-oz) lemonade,Frozen -concentrate,thawed

- ❖ 1 cn (6-oz) limeade,Frozen -concentrate,thawed

- ❖ 1 cn (6-oz) orange juice,Frozen -concentrate, thawed

- ❖ 2 pk (10-oz) sliced,Frozen -strawberries,thawed

- ❖ 3 c cold water

- ❖ 1 bottle (2-liter) ginger ale - chilled

Combine the first 5 ingredients; add the ginger ale, and stir gently. Makes 1 gallon, serves about 12.

➤STRAWBERRY-LIME PUNCH

Yield 1 Servings

- ❖ 1 1/2 c pineapple juice
- ❖ 1/2 c orange juice
- ❖ 2 T lime juice
- ❖ 1/2 c sugar
- ❖ 1 pk sliced strawberries,Frozen
- ❖ -thawed (10 oz.)
- ❖ 1 l lemon-lime soda,chilled
- ❖ Fresh fruit for,Slices -garnish

In 2-quart pitcher, combine pineapple juice, orange juice, lime juice and sugar; stir until sugar is dissolved. Stir in strawberries.

Refrigerate until ready to serve. To serve, stir in soda; pour into glasses. Garnish with fruit slices, if desired.

➤SUMMER CITRUS PUNCH

Yield 13 Servings

- ❖ 7 c orange juice
- ❖ 3 c vodka
- ❖ 1 1/2 c grapefnuit juice
- ❖ 3/4 c fresh lime juice
- ❖ 3/4 c fresh lemon juice
- ❖ 1/3 c sugar
- ❖ 50 ice cubes
- ❖ 1 orange,sliced
- ❖ 1 lemon,sliced
- ❖ 1 pt strawberries
- ❖ 1 additional ice cubes

Combine first to ingredients in punch bowl. Stir until sugar dissolves. Add 50 ice cubes, orange slices, lemon slices and berries and stir gently to combine. Fill glasses with add it ice. Ladle punch into glasses and serve.

➤SUMMER PUNCH

Yield 10 Servings

- ❖ 2 l white wine,chilled
- ❖ 1 l club soda,chilled
- ❖ 3 oz brandy
- ❖ 3 oz orange liqueur
- ❖ 1 c strong tea
- ❖ 3 lemons,juice
- ❖ 2 limes,juice

Pour into punch bowl over block of ice. Garnish with sliced fruit and mint sprigs. Ideal for showers or anniversary parties

➤SUMMERTIME FRUIT PUNCH

Yield 1 Servings

- ❖ 1 orange,grated rind of
- ❖ 1lemon,grated rind of
- ❖ 2 2 c wate
- ❖ 3 c sugar
- ❖ 2 t almond extract
- ❖ 2c orange juice,fresh,straind
- ❖ 1/2 c lemon juice,fresh,strained
- ❖ 48 oz cranberry juice cocktail
- ❖ 1 qt ginger ale

Combine orange and lemon rind, water, and sugar in a medium saucepan.

Bring to a boil, and simmer 5 minutes; let cool. Stir in almond extract and fruit juice. Pour over ice; stir in ginger ale.

➤SUMMERTIME PUNCH

Yield 1 Servings

- ❖ 2 c watermelon,cubed

- ❖ 1 orange

Peel orange and prepare watermelon according to your juicer's instructions. Pour over crushed ice, shake, and strain juice into glasses.

➤SUNNY HOLIDAY PUNCH

Yield 1 Servings

- ❖ 46 oz can pineapple juice,chilled

- ❖ 28 oz bottle mineral water (or-club) - soda,chilled

- ❖ 6 oz can orange juice,Frozen -concentrate

- ❖ 1lemon (or lime),thinly -sliced

- ❖ 2 c fresh (or berries),Frozen 750 ml champagne,chilled

Combine all ingredients in a punch bowl. Garnish as desired.

➤SUNSET PUNCH

Yield 1 Servings

- ❖ 1 2 liter bott Schweppes
  -Raspberry Gingerale

- ❖ 1 46 ounce can Apricot Nectar

- ❖ 1 qt Sherbet- orange,raspberry,

- ❖ -lemon,or trop.fruit

Basic recipe is 1 part Apricot Nectar to 2 or 2 1/2 parts Raspberry Gingerale. Top with scoop(s) of sherbet.

➤SUNSHINE PUNCH

Yield 12 Servings

- ❖ 3 c orange juice - unsweetened
- ❖ 1 cn 12 oz. unsweetened pineapple juice
- ❖ 1/2 c lemon juice
- ❖ 1 artificial sweetener equal
- ❖ -to 1/2 c,up sugar
- ❖ 16 oz bottle sugar free lemon lime - (or gin),ger ale

Combine all ingredients except soda. Chill. Add pop just before serving. This is really attractive if served with ice molded in a jello mold or block with with orange slices.

➤SWAMP WATER PUNCH

Yield 1 Servings

- ❖ 1 orange juice

- ❖ 1 optional ginger ale,alcohol of some kind

- ❖ 1 blue food coloring

- ❖ 1 optional floating

- ❖ ARM OF DEATH

- ❖ 1 water (or orange juice)

- ❖ 1 optional,gummy worms

Put some blue food coloring into the orange juice punch until it turns a disgusting swamp-green color. The color is gross and the orange juice pulp floating around really adds to the effect. People will realize that the punch tastes good, but it will take them awhile to figure out it is orange juice.

Floating Arm-of-Death Freeze the water (and gummy worms if desired) in a clean rubber glove. Peel off the rubber glove and float the arm in the punch.

➤SWEET CIDER PUNCH

Yield 20 Servings

- ❖ 1 c sugar
- ❖ 2 c water
- ❖ 3 lemons
- ❖ 1 qt sweet cider
- ❖ 2 c grape juice

Place sugar in water and boil for about 10 minutes, adding a little of the outer rind of a lemon. When cold, add lemon juice, then add the sweet cider and place in refrigerator and freeze to mushy consistency. When frozen, mix in grape juice. Serve in tall glasses.

➤TAHITIAN PUNCH

Yield 1 Servings

- ❖ 1 cn pineapple juice,chilled

- ❖ 21 cn orange-grapefruit juice -chilled

- ❖ 3 qt carbonated lemon-lime

- ❖ -beverage,chilled

- ❖ 1 pt lemon (or lime sherbet)

In punch bowl, stir together juices and carbonated beverage. Spoon sherbet into bowl. Serve immediately.

➤TAMARIND PUNCH WITH SATAYS

Yield 1 Servings

- ❖ PUNCH
- ❖ part tamarind water
- ❖ 2 T lime juice
- ❖ parts brown sugar
- ❖ parts dark rum
- ❖ parts lemonade
- ❖ 1 pinches mace
- ❖ 1 ice
- ❖ SATAYS
- ❖ 1 sirloin steak
- ❖ 1 chicken breast
- ❖ 12 prawns,Cooked
- ❖ 1 t vegetable oil
- ❖ 1 t turmeric

To make the punch mix all the ingredients together and serve with ice. To make the satays, fry the meat and fish until brown, separately in oil with turmeric. Serve with the punch.

➤TEA AND FRUIT PUNCH

Yield 1 Servings

- ❖ 6 apples,peeled and sliced

- ❖ 4 bananas,peeled and sliced

- ❖ 8 oz seedless grapes (or),Halved and pitted

- ❖ 1,grapes

- ❖ 4 pt water

- ❖ 1 1/2 lb sugar

- ❖ 5 oranges,

- ❖ juice of 5 lemons,

- ❖ juice of 1 pt ginger ale

- ❖ 1/2 pt cold tea (or herbal tea)

- ❖ 1 1/2 pt soda water

- ❖ 1 bottle gin (or vodka) -(optional)

1. Put the fruit in a punch bowl.

2. Heat the water in a pan and dissolve the sugar and the fruit

juice, stir well and simmer for 5 minutes. Pour over the fruit and set aside to cool.

3. Just before serving, add the ginger ale, tea, soda water and alcohol.

➤TEA PUNCH

Yield 20 Servings

- ❖ 3 c tea,strong

- ❖ 4 1 c lemon juice

- ❖ 5 c orange juice

- ❖ 2 c raspberry syrup,or grenadin

- ❖ 1 c pineapple,crushed

- ❖ 1 sugar,to taste

- ❖ 2 qt club soda,chilled

Combine all ingredients except club soda in a punch bowl with a large block of clear ice; allow to chill thoroughly. (If fresh fruit juices are used, they should be strained.) Add club soda just before serving.

➤TEMPERANCE PUNCH

Yield 1 Servings

- ❖ 2 cn frozen orange juice,large
- ❖ 3cn frozen lemonade,large
- ❖ 8cn water
- ❖ 2c grenadine
- ❖ 3 1/2 c lemon juice
- ❖ 4 qt ginger ale,chilled

Mix together; float orange slices on top. Add cherries.

➤TEXAS GOLDEN PUNCH

Yield 125 Servings

- ❖ 4 cn (12-oz) orange juice,Frozen
- ❖ 5 4 cn (12-oz) lemonade,Frozen
- ❖ 4 cn (46-oz) pineapple juice
- ❖ 4 cn (46-oz) apple juice
- ❖ 4 bottles ginger ale

Combine orange juice & lemonade using only half as much water as directed on the cans. Add pineapple juice & apple juice. Mix well & freeze.

Remove from freezer 3 hours before serving. It should be slushy when ready to serve. Add ginger ale. Serves about 125.

➤THE "PUNCH"

Yield 20 Servings

- ❖ 1 l Sprite

- ❖ 1 l 7-up®

- ❖ 8 oz Orange Juice,Frozen -Concentrate

- ❖ 6 Scoops Country Time Lemonade

- ❖ 1c Sugar

- ❖ 1 l Water

- ❖ 46 oz Unsweetened Pineapple Juice

Thoroughly combine ingredients and serve over lots of crushed ice.

➤THE BRIDAL SWEET PUNCH

Yield 48 Servings

- ❖ 10 tea bags
- ❖ 3 c sugar
- ❖ 3 c orange juice
- ❖ 3 c pineapple juice,unsweetened
- ❖ 1 c lemon juice,fresh,strained
- ❖ 2 qt ginger ale
- ❖ GARNISH
- ❖ 1 mint leaves

Bring the water to a boil, add the tea bags and steep for 5 minutes. Remove the tea bags, add the sugar, mix and chill for at least 3 hours. Place the chilled tea in a punch bowl, add the juices, and stir. Just before serving, add the ginger ale and stir. Add some ice cubes and garnish with mint leaves.

➤THREE FRUIT PUNCH

Yield 20 Servings

- ❖ 1 qt Pineapple juice,chilled

- ❖ 1qt Orange juice,chilled

- ❖ 11/2 qt Cranberry cocktail juice -chilled

- ❖ 3l Ginger ale,chilled

- ❖ 3Starfruit,cut 1/4" slices

- ❖ 4 Ice cubes (or an ice ring)

- ❖ distilled water with gummy -worms

In a large punch bowl combine pineapple, orange, cranberry juices and ginger ale. Stir in starfruit slices. Add ice or ice ring. Serve chilled.This recipe yields approximately 20 servings.

➤TIGER PAUSE PUNCH

Yield 20 Servings

- ❖ 1/2 ga Orange Sherbet

- ❖ 2 l Ginger Ale

- ❖ 1 l Soda Water

Pour ingredients into punch bowl. Garnish with cherries and/or mint sprigs.

➤TRINITY WEDDING PUNCH

Yield 25 Servings

- ❖ 2 qt 7 up,chilled

- ❖ 1 pt sherbet (flavor color)

- ❖ 12 oz lemonade,undiluted

Soften sherbet, stir in lemonade that is partially thawed. Pour in 7-up and serve.

➤TROPICAL CHAMPAGNE PUNCH

Yield 50 Servings

- ❖ 2 ct (8 oz. each) guava,Frozen -mango juice drink conc.

- ❖ 2 ct (8 oz. each) kiwi,Frozen -strawberry,juice drink conc.

- ❖ 4 bottles,(1 liter each) club -soda

- ❖ 6 bottles,(750 ml each) champagne

Shortly before serving combine all ingredients and mix thoroughly.

➤TROPICAL FRUIT PUNCH

Yield 1 Servings

- ❖ 1 carton,(64-ounce)
  -pine-orange

- ❖ 1 bottle,(32-ounce)
  -lemon-lime soda

- ❖ 1 cn (6-ounce) limeade,Frozen
  -concentrate, thawed

- ❖ 1 pk (16-ounce) peaches,Frozen

- ❖ 1 pk (12-ounce),Frozen raspberries

- ❖ 2 firm bananas,, peeled and sliced

- ❖ 2 oranges,, peeled and sliced

Combine all ingredients in a punch bowl. Stir and serve Recipe by Makes 28 (4-ounce) servings

➤TROPICAL PUNCH

Yield 1 Servings

- ❖ 2 c bananas,Mashed

- ❖ 1 can(20oz.),Crushed
  -pineapple,undrained

- ❖ 1 jar(4oz.) maraschino cherries,drained and chopp

- ❖ 2 c orange juice

- ❖ 1 T lemon juice

- ❖ 1 c sugar

- ❖ 33 3/4 oz ginger ale,(1 bottle)

Combine first six ingredients; stir well, and freeze until firm. To

serve, partially thaw fruit mixture. Place in punch bowl, and break

into chunks. Add ginger ale and stir until slushy.

Makes 12 cups.

➤TUTTI-FRUTTI PUNCH

Yield 1 Servings

- ❖ 16 oz pkg frozen strawberries,thaw
- ❖ 6 oz froz pineapple juice,thaw
- ❖ 3 oz froz apple juice,thaw
- ❖ 3 oz froz orange juice,thaw
- ❖ 1 1/2 c water
- ❖ 33 oz bottle seltzer,chilled

Combine first 4 ingredients in container of blender; procees until smooth. Combine strawberry mixture and water in a large pitcher; cover and chill at least 3 hours. To serve, add seltzer to juice mixture and stir gently. Serve punch immediately.

➤U-238 PUNCH

Yield 40 Servings

- ❖ 1 qt rum
- ❖ 1 qt vodka
- ❖ 1 qt strawberry juice
- ❖ 1 qt orange juice
- ❖ 1 qt pineapple juice
- ❖ 1 pt fresh strawberries
- ❖ 1 pt orange wedges
- ❖ 1 pt pineapple chunks

Mix all ingredients well. Chill. Serve as you would punch.

➤ULTIMATE PUNCH

Yield 10 Servings

- ❖ 1 5th champagne

- ❖ 1 qt Ginger ale

- ❖ 1 pk strawbewrries,Frozen

- ❖ 1 pk raspberries,Frozen

- ❖ 1 qt Vanilla ice cream

- ❖ 1 qt Lemon sherbet -OR-
  -raspberry

Prepare about 1/2 hour prior to serving. Mix all ingredients together until ice cream and sherbet are liquified; do not use blender. Don't use lemon-lime sherbert the green coloring will give the punch an ugly beige cast. Punch should appear white and pink.

➤VALENTINE'S DAY PUNCH

Yield 1 Servings

- ❖ 2 c chilled grape juice
- ❖ 3 4 c chilled orange juice
- ❖ 4 8 c ginger ale
- ❖ 1/4 c sugar
- ❖ 2 oranges

Mix all ingredients except oranges. Peel oranges and remove all seeds. Float orange pieces on top. Chill and serve.

➤VAMPIRE PUNCH

Yield 1 Servings

- ❖ 8 c cranberry juice

- ❖ 6 c sparkling apple cider

- ❖ 6 orange,Slices

Put all ingredients in a punch bowl. Add ice cubes just before serving.

MAKES 14 CUPS

➤VITELLO TONNATO ; IMPERIAL PUNCH

Yield 22 Servings

- ❖ 3 c water
- ❖ ½ vanilla beans
- ❖ 1 sm cinnamon stick
- ❖ 1 c sugar
- ❖ 1 sl lemon,peeled
- ❖ 1 sl orange,peeled
- ❖ 1 13 1/2ounce can pineapple
- ❖ -tidbits,drained (1 cup)
- ❖ 4 oranges,peeled and sectioned
- ❖ 6 lemon,juice
- ❖ 2 1pint 7Oz bottles Rhine wine
- ❖ 2 c kirsch liqueur
- ❖ 1 4/5-quart bottle champagne -chilled

Combine water, vanilla bean, cinnamon stick, sugar and lemon and orange rind in a saucepan. Bring to a bol for two minutes. Chill; strain into punch bowl. Add pineapple tidbits, diced orange, lemon juice wine and kirsch. Cover bowl and chill for several hours. Add champagne just before serving.

Makes about one gallon or enough for 22 (3/4) cup servings

➤VODKA PUNCH

Yield 28 Servings

- ❖ 1 qt cranberry juice

- ❖ 2 c vodka

- ❖ 1 cn 6 oz. lemonade,Frozen

- ❖ 1 1/2 qt 7-up,chilled (48 oz.)

Combine all ingredients in punch bowl. Chill with an ice ring. Makes 28 - 4 oz. drinks.

➤VOODOO PUNCH

Yield 32 Servings

- ❖ 3/4 c light brown sugar,Packed
- ❖ 1 3-inch piece fresh ginger
- ❖ 2 T peppercorns,whole
- ❖ 1 T allspice,whole
- ❖ 4 cinnamon sticks
- ❖ 2 c water
- ❖ 1 large block of ice
- ❖ 26 oz dark caribbean rum
- ❖ 26 oz vodka
- ❖ 2 c orange juice
- ❖ 1/2 c pineapple juice
- ❖ 10 flowers,see note
- ❖ 10 lemon,Slices

Peel ginger and slice thinly. In a 1-quart saucepan, combine brown sugar, ginger, peppercorns, allspice, cinnamon sticks and water. Bring to boil; then reduce heat and simmer, uncovered, 30 minutes.

Strain, discarding spices; chill. If made ahead, set aside until ready to use. To prepare punch for serving place ice block (should be 2 quarts) in punch bowl. Add chilled syrup, rum, vodka, orange juice and pineapple juice. Taste and add more juices, if desired. Poke stem of each flower through the center of a lemon slice; float slices atop punch. Serve each drink over ice cubes.

➤WARM BUTTERED RUM PUNCH

Yield 1 Servings

- ❖ 6 T dark brown sugar

- ❖ 100 g unsalted butter,(4oz)

- ❖ 1/4 t nutmeg

- ❖ 1/4 t nutmeg

- ❖ 1/4 t cloves,Ground

- ❖ 1 mandarin (or tangerine),zest of

- ❖ ½ lemon,zest of

- ❖ 125 ml dark rum,(4fl oz)

Place the sugar and butter into a heavy based pan and stir until dissolved. Carefully add all the other ingredients to the butter and sugar mix and bring to the boil, stirring well. Simmer gently for 2-3 minutes and turn off the heat. Leave to cool slightly.

Pour into glasses or mugs and serve.

➤WARM TEA PUNCH

Yield 8 Servings

- ❖ 1 1/2 c water
- ❖ 6 orange herbal tea bags
- ❖ 10 hole cloves
- ❖ 2 cinnamon sticks
- ❖ 2 c cranberry juice
- ❖ 1 1/2 c white grape juice
- ❖ 1/2 c brown sugar,Packed
- ❖ 1 orange/whole cloves--,Slices
- ❖ optional for garnish

In a medium saucepan, bring water to a boil. Turn off heat; add tea bags, cloves and cinnamon sticks. Cover and steep for 5 minutes. Remove tea bags. Stir in the juices and brown sugar; heat through. Remove spices. Garnish with clove-studded orange slices if desired.

➤ZESTY PUNCH SIPPER

Yield 6 Servings

- ❖ 2 bottles ginger ale,chilled,

- ❖ 32-ounces each

- ❖ 6 c pineapple (or orange juice) -chilled

- ❖ 1 (6 ounce) can,Frozen lemonade concentrate,

- ❖ 1 orange,thinly sliced for garnish (optional)

- ❖ 1 lime,thinly sliced, for garnish (optional)

Combine all ingredients in a large punch bowl or two large pitchers.

9 788367 110297